Web Programming with Go

Building and Scaling Interactive Web Applications with Go's Robust Ecosystem

Ian Taylor

Copyright © 2023 by GitforGits

All rights reserved. This book is protected under copyright laws and no part of it may be reproduced or transmitted in any form or by any means, electronic or mechanical, including photocopying, recording, or by any information storage and retrieval system, without the prior written permission of the publisher. Any unauthorized reproduction, distribution, or transmission of this work may result in civil and criminal penalties and will be dealt with in the respective jurisdiction at anywhere in India, in accordance with the applicable copyright laws.

Published by: GitforGits
Publisher: Sonal Dhandre
www.gitforgits.com
support@gitforgits.com

Printed in India

First Printing: October 2023

ISBN: 9788119177943

Cover Design by: Kitten Publishing

For permission to use material from this book, please contact GitforGits at support@gitforgits.com.

Prologue

With new online technologies appearing seemingly out of nowhere, developers in this day must choose a language that can include speed, reliability, and efficiency into their work. This is where "Web Programming with Go" comes in, taking you on a comprehensive journey through the huge universe of Go's web capabilities.

Go, or Golang as it is generally called, did not emerge by chance. It was a purposeful design by tech titans who saw a hole in the linguistic landscape and felt compelled to fill it with a language that was current, succinct, and innately equipped to deal with the issues of today's multithreaded online environments. Go was created with a concept in mind: to simplify the complex and emphasize the important, making it a joy for developers to choreograph programs that were not only functional, but also performative.

"Web Programming with Go" is more than simply a how-to guide for functions, loops, and libraries; it's a manifesto for modern web programming. Each chapter peels back the layers of Go, guaranteeing that by the end, you have not only comprehended but also assimilated its philosophy. It is necessary to comprehend the why before the how. Why Go favors composition over inheritance, why Go's concurrency model is its finest achievement, and why Go could be the language you didn't realize you needed.

This book's underpinning strength is its hands-on methodology. We believe in learning by doing, so a constant thread of a practical example - our beloved 'bookstore app' - runs through the book's tapestry. It, like you, evolves, grows, and scales. Our bookshop software stands as a tribute to the strength of Go, moving from a primitive model into a state-of-the-art application with each chapter as we delve into subjects ranging from routing mechanics to API integrations.

The modern web is about more than just retrieving and presenting data; it's about integrating with a plethora of services, providing dynamic user experiences, scaling on the fly, and, most critically, ensuring performance doesn't deteriorate even while under strain. As you read this book, you'll notice Go standing tall, a beacon guiding you through these difficulties. You'll learn how to use Go's power to make sure your applications aren't simply useful, but also fast.

Another noteworthy aspect of this book is its in-depth examination of debugging and performance evaluation. Debugging is more than just finding mistakes; it's about understanding your application, identifying its pain points, and addressing them. Go's vast toolkit makes this once-difficult operation practically intuitive, and this book assures you're well-prepared to employ every tool in Go's arsenal.

We hope you find "Web Programming with Go" not only instructive but also transforming as you embark on this adventure. Whether you're a seasoned coder, an enthusiast, or someone at a crossroads of languages unsure which path to choose, this book aims to be your compass, guide, and, at times, mentor. As you turn the page, you're not just beginning a new chapter; you're embarking on what we promise will be an exciting journey into the world of Go. Have fun coding!

Content

Preface xiii
CHAPTER 1: INTRODUCTION TO WEB DEVELOPMENT IN GO 1
   Introduction to Web Development 2
   Opportunities for Go 3
   Go Toolchain 5
      Compiler 6
      Dependency and Package Management 6
      Testing and Benchmarking 7
   Setting up Go on Linux 7
      Installing Go 7
      Configuring Go Workspace 8
      Introducing Go Modules 8
      Setting up Tools and Libraries 9
      IDE and Code Editors 9
   net/http Package 10
      net/http Overview 10
      HTTP Servers and Clients 10
      Handlers and HandlerFuncs 11
      Routing Requests 11
      Data Request and Response 11
      Using net/http 11
   Introducing Bookstore Web Application 12
   Go RESTful Services 14
      Key Principles of REST 14
      Implementing RESTful Services with Go 15
      Go's Advantage in RESTful Development 16
   Building my First Web Server 16
      Initializing Project 16

  Crafting Basic Server 17
  Running the Server 18
 Summary 18

Chapter 2: Structuring Go Web Application 20

 Explore Go Modules 21
  Essence of Go Modules 21
  Transitioning to Modules 21
  Dependency Management with Modules 22
  Understanding Module Proxies 23
 Standard Go Directory Structure 23
  Designing Directory Structure 24
 Package Management and Vendoring 26
  Why Package Management Matters? 27
  Need of Vendoring 27
  Implementing Package Management 29
 Model-View-Controller (MVC) in Go 30
  Understanding MVC 30
  Benefits of MVC 30
  Applying MVC to GitforGits Bookstore 31
 Programming Main Application Object 33
  Defining Application Object Structure 33
  Crafting Main Application Object 33
  Decoding the Script 35
 Configuration and Environment Variables 35
  Implementing Configuration and Environment Variables 36
 Dependency Injection 38
  Overview 38
  Benefits of Dependency Injection 38
  Implementing Dependency Injection 39
 Health Check Endpoints 40
  Setting up Health Check Endpoints 40

Summary 42
Chapter 3: Handling HTTP Requests and Routing 43
Backbone of Web 44
    HTTP Requests and Routing 44
    HTTP Methods 44
Navigate User Interactions 45
    Request-Response Paradigm 45
    Request Phase 45
    Response Phase 45
Handlers and HandlerFuncs 46
    Understanding HandlerFuncs 46
Explore Routes 48
    Routes as Connectors 48
    Route Patterns and Dynamic Routing 48
    Route Grouping and Hierarchical Routing 49
Routes Programming 49
    Setting up Routes 49
    Dynamic Routes and Route Variables 49
    Middleware in Routing 50
    Error Handling and Custom 404 Pages 50
URL Parameters 51
    Types of URL Parameters 51
    Implementing Dynamic URL Parameters 52
Grouping Routes 53
    Overview 53
    Sample Program: Structuring Endpoints 53
Navigate Web Routing with Gorilla/Mux 55
    Setting up Gorilla/Mux 55
    Configuring Gorilla/Mux for Optimal Performance 57
Error Handling in Go 57
    404 Not Found Error 58

  500 Internal Server Error 58

 Rate Limiting and Request Throttling 59

  Overview 59

  Rate Limiting for GitforGits Bookstore 60

 Performing CRUD Operations 61

  Creating Book 61

  Reading Book Details 62

  Updating Book 62

  Deleting Book 63

 Summary 64

Chapter 4: Templating and Rendering Content **65**

 Dynamic Rendering Overview 66

 Templates Deep Dive 67

  Symphony of Variables 67

  Loops 67

  Conditions 67

 Nested Templates in Action 68

  Constructing the Framework 68

  Carving the Header 69

  Crafting the Content 69

  Sealing the Footer 70

 Design Main Page Layout 70

  Structuring Base Layout 71

  Designing Header 71

  Building Dynamic Content Area 72

  Outlining Holistic Footer 73

 Handling Forms and User Inputs 74

  Laying Groundwork 74

  Dropdowns, Radios, and Checkboxes 74

  Validation 75

  Processing Form Data 75

- Template Caching ... 76
  - Overview ... 76
  - Go's Template Package ... 76
  - Deploying Cached Templates ... 77
- Safe HTML Rendering ... 77
  - Need for Safe Rendering ... 77
  - Cross-Site Scripting (XSS) ... 77
  - Contextual Encoding ... 78
- Template Debugging ... 79
  - Scenario#1: Malformed Templates ... 79
  - Scenario#2: Missing or Mismatched Data ... 79
  - Scenario#3: Incorrect Logic or Conditions ... 80
- Summary ... 81

Chapter 5: Interaction with Databases ... 82
- Introduction to Persistent Storage ... 83
- database/sql Package ... 84
  - Overview ... 84
  - Install Drivers ... 84
  - Connecting Database ... 84
  - Crafting and Executing Queries ... 85
  - Insertions, Updates, and Deletions ... 85
  - Managing Database Connections ... 86
- Sample Program: Design Robust Database ... 86
  - Nature of Data ... 86
  - Books as Core Entity ... 86
  - Categorizing Books as Genres ... 87
  - Users ... 87
  - Book Reviews ... 87
  - Transactions ... 88
  - Inventory Management ... 88
- Leverage ORMs ... 89

- Strengthen Database Indexing 90
  - Primary Indexing 90
  - Secondary Indexing 90
  - Primary vs. Secondary Indexes 90
  - Composite Indexes 91
  - Covering Indexes 91
  - Partial Indexes 91
- Manage Database Connections 92
  - Connection Pooling 92
  - Integrating Connection Pooling 92
  - Tuning Connection Pool 92
  - Connection Health Checks 93
- Advanced SQL Queries 93
  - Joins 93
  - Subqueries 94
  - Aggregations 94
- Summary 96

Chapter 6: Concurrency in Go **97**
- Age of Rapid Applications 98
  - Concurrency for Parallel Execution 98
  - Go's Concurrency Paradigm 98
- Go's Goroutines 99
  - Understanding Goroutines 99
  - Sample Program: Concurrent Book Searches 99
- Goroutines Channeling 101
  - Need of Channels 101
  - Using Channels 101
  - Buffered Channels 102
  - Closing Channels 102
  - Multiplexing Channel Operations 102
- Up and Running with Synchronization 103

Importance of Synchronization	103
sync.WaitGroup	103
sync.Mutex	104
Combining WaitGroup and Mutex	105
Implement Concurrent Cache	106
Parallelism vs. Concurrency	108
Unveiling Parallelism	108
Sample Program: Book Recommendation Function	108
Do's and Don'ts	109
Summary	111
Chapter 7: Sessions, Authentication, and Authorization	**112**
User Sessions Overview	113
Store Session Data	114
Session Storage Options	114
Secure Cookie Handling	116
Secure Cookies Overview	116
Implementing HTTPOnly Attribute	116
Secure Cookies with Secure Attribute	116
SameSite Attribute	117
Encrypting Cookie Values	117
Implement User Authentication	118
Setting up Database	118
Registering New User	118
Logging In an Existing User	119
Managing User Sessions	119
Logging Out User	119
Protect and Secure User Passwords	120
Hashing	120
Salting	120
Pepper	121
Iterations	121

  Up-to-date Algorithms 121
 Implement and Operate OAuth 122
  Understanding OAuth 122
  Setting up OAuth 122
  Redirection and Callbacks 123
 Summary 123

Chapter 8: Frontend and Backend Communication 125
 Frontend-Backend Overview 126
 RESTful API Overview 127
  Background 127
  Stateless Interactions 127
  Client-Server Architecture 127
  Uniform Interface 127
  Layered System 128
  State Representations 128
 Build My First API 128
  Project Initialization and Import Packages 128
  Defining Book Structure 128
  Sample Data 129
  Creating Endpoint Function 129
  Setting up Server 130
  Testing Endpoint 130
 JSON and Its Importance 130
  Basic JSON Structure 131
 Program Data Fetching 132
  Setting up Endpoint 132
  Interacting with Database 132
 Goroutines and Channels for Data Fetching 134
  Why Concurrency in Data Fetching? 134
  Sample Program: Concurrent Data Fetching 135
 Authenticating APIs 136

- Importance of API Security 136
- What is API Authentication? 136
- Using API Tokens for Authentication 137
- Generating and Validating Tokens 137
- Middleware for Authentication 138
- Integrate External APIs 139
  - Choose and Communicate Third-Party API 139
  - Sample Program: Integration of Payment Gateway 140
- Summary 141

Chapter 9: Testing and Debugging 142
- Testing and Debugging Overview 143
- Go Testing Package 143
  - Fundamentals 143
  - Powerful Assertions and Flow Control 144
  - Performance Benchmarks 145
  - Testing Web Applications 145
- Initiating Testing 146
  - Setting up Environment 146
  - Test File Structure 147
  - Fetching a Book 147
  - Executing Test 148
  - Refining Test with Mock Data 148
  - Enhancing Test 148
- Handling Multiple Test Cases 149
  - Table-Driven Testing 149
  - Utilizing Helper Functions 150
  - Parallel Testing 151
  - Subtests 151
- Mock Dependencies 152
  - Introduction to Mocking 152
  - Why Mock Dependencies? 152

- Creating Mock Database 152
  - Using Mock in Tests 153
- Tracing and Logging 154
  - Performing Logging with Go's log 155
  - Integrating Advanced Logging Libraries 155
  - Error Tracing 156
- Application Performance Profiling 157
  - CPU Profiling 157
  - Block Profiling 157
  - Memory Profiling 158
- Errors and Troubleshooting 158
  - N+1 Query Problem 158
  - Data Race Conditions 159
  - Memory Leaks 159
  - Broken Authentication Flows 160
  - Inefficient Data Handling 160
  - Input Validation Failures 160
  - Incorrect Error Handling 161
  - Dependency Update Failure 161
  - Hardcoding Configuration 161
  - Unsafe Concurrency Handling 162
- Summary 162
- **Index** 165
- **Epilogue** 167

Preface

"Web Programming with Go" is a must-have book for software professionals and web developers looking to harness Go's potential for creating excellent web apps. The extensive knowledge imparted by this book about Go's powerful libraries and packages is crucial for building scalable and efficient web platforms.

The book's core focus is on exploring deeply into the complexities of web development through the perspective of Go. The first step in building any web application is to review the fundamentals, which will serve as a foundation for the rest of the learning experience. As you explore deeper, you'll learn about the diverse ecosystem that supports Go. This ecosystem covers a wide range of issues, including the complexities of routing mechanics, HTTP requests, and Go's concurrency model, all with the goal of improving web efficiency.

The book uses the example of a "bookstore app" throughout the book, providing you with a practical touchpoint on every possible learning. With this iterative example, you can follow the development of a simple web app from its infancy all the way to a fully featured, robust platform.

The later sections of the book focus on performance evaluation and debugging, which are frequently overlooked in other Go books. This book takes you from the fundamentals of web development to the depths of Go, culminating in a strong online application designed to meet today's digital issues. This book promises to be your compass in the vast ocean of web development, whether you're an experienced developer or an enthusiast just getting started with Go.

In this book you will learn how to:

- Master Go's efficient syntax and streamline coding with better performance.
- Build robust web applications from scratch, ensuring scalability and responsiveness.
- Seamlessly integrate APIs, enhancing app functionality and user experience.
- Harness Go's concurrency, boosting app speed and multitasking capabilities.
- Optimize data storage and retrieval with Go, ensuring data integrity and speed.
- Develop resilient apps by mastering error detection and troubleshooting in Go.
- Implement user sessions, enhancing user experience and data security.
- Ensure app reliability through Go's comprehensive testing and debugging techniques.
- Utilize Go tools for real-time performance tracking, ensuring optimal user experiences.
- Safeguard user data and interactions through Go's top-tier security practices.

GitforGits

Prerequisites

Targeted at experienced programmers in other languages and Go beginners interested in mastering web application development, and professionals seeking to update their web development toolkit with Go.

Codes Usage

Are you in need of some helpful code examples to assist you in your programming and documentation? Look no further! Our book offers a wealth of supplemental material, including code examples and exercises.

Not only is this book here to aid you in getting your job done, but you have our permission to use the example code in your programs and documentation. However, please note that if you are reproducing a significant portion of the code, we do require you to contact us for permission.

But don't worry, using several chunks of code from this book in your program or answering a question by citing our book and quoting example code does not require permission. But if you do choose to give credit, an attribution typically includes the title, author, publisher, and ISBN. For example, "Web Programming with Go by Ian Taylor".

If you are unsure whether your intended use of the code examples falls under fair use or the permissions outlined above, please do not hesitate to reach out to us at support@gitforgits.com.

We are happy to assist and clarify any concerns.

Acknowledgement

I owe a tremendous debt of gratitude to GitforGits, for their unflagging enthusiasm and wise counsel throughout the entire process of writing this book. Their knowledge and careful editing helped make sure the piece was useful for people of all reading levels and comprehension skills. In addition, I'd like to thank everyone involved in the publishing process for their efforts in making this book a reality. Their efforts, from copyediting to advertising, made the project what it is today.

Finally, I'd like to express my gratitude to everyone who has shown me unconditional love and encouragement throughout my life. Their support was crucial to the completion of this book. I appreciate your help with this endeavour and your continued interest in my career.

Chapter 1: Introduction to Web Development in Go

Introduction to Web Development

In 2007, Robert Griesemer, Rob Pike, and Ken Thompson at Google came up with the idea for the Go programming language, which is also referred to as Golang. Their intention was to address the complexities and deficiencies that they saw in other languages. What began as an exploratory project with the intention of resolving common criticisms of popular languages such as C++ and Java, particularly in terms of scalability and concurrency, eventually resulted in the release of Go 1.0 in the year 2012. Not only was this a watershed moment in the history of the language, but it was also a watershed moment from the perspective of web development. The introduction of Go into the sphere of web development was, in many ways, like a breath of fresh air. In an environment that was dominated by languages that either required a significant learning curve or were unable to handle the growing demand for concurrent processing in an efficient manner, the simplicity and power of Go stood out. As a result of its inherent concurrency support, which was provided by goroutines, channels, and the select statement, the game was completely transformed. The combination of these features, along with the fact that Go is a statically-typed language and has the efficiency of a compiled language, made it a viable option for web backends that required rapid performance, scalability, and the capacity to handle thousands of requests at the same time.

In the universe of web development, the proliferation of microservices has further accelerated the adoption of Go. It was necessary for businesses to have a method by which they could construct small, independent services that could be independently developed, deployed, and scaled. Go's built-in support for concurrent processing, along with its minimalistic design and lightning-fast execution, makes it an ideal fit for the microservices paradigm. Web developers were also drawn to its standard library because it offered a wide variety of utilities for web servers, database connections, and data handling right out of the box. This was another major attraction for web developers. Instead of having to navigate through dozens of different middleware and external libraries, developers could accomplish a great deal with just the standard library, which would make web projects more straightforward and improve their overall efficiency.

The Go ecosystem has flourished over the years, which has resulted in the introduction of a multitude of third-party packages and frameworks that are specifically designed for web development. These third-party tools provided more specialized functionalities, which filled in gaps and catered to niche requirements. While the standard library was sufficient for many, these tools offered more customized functionalities. It is widely acknowledged that the Go community, which is known for its collaborative efforts and active participation, was a significant contributor to this expansion. Package managers such as 'dep' and later 'Go Modules' simplified dependency management, which was one of the most significant challenges that developers had to deal with. Some libraries, such as Gorilla Mux, added sophisticated routing capabilities, while others, such as GORM, provided an ORM layer for Go, which simplified database operations.

An additional factor that contributed significantly to Go's widespread adoption was the fact that it is compatible and works well with a variety of other languages and platforms. Businesses were able to experience smoother transitions as a result of the ease with which Go services could interact with components written in other languages. Through the utilization of this hybrid approach, organizations were able to experiment with Go for particular services without having to completely revamp their technology stack.

Go's deployment advantage was another significant factor that contributed to its rise to prominence in the web development landscape. Applications written in Go are compiled into a single binary file, which contains all of the dependencies. Because of this, there was no longer a requirement for external runtime environments, which simplified deployments and reduced the likelihood of problems resulting from missing or mismatched dependencies. In the modern era of containerization and orchestration tools such as Docker and Kubernetes, the single binary advantage of Go ensures that container sizes are reduced and deployment times are sped up.

On the other hand, the acceptance of Go in web development was not solely due to its exceptional technical capabilities. Go's fundamental philosophy, which places an emphasis on readability and simplicity, struck a chord with a great number of people. Because Go's syntax is so concise, codebases were much simpler to maintain, and the likelihood of bugs making their way into the system was significantly reduced. There was an increase in the efficiency of code reviews, and the process of integrating new team members into projects was simplified. The essence of Go is that it not only offered the tools necessary for the development of robust web applications, but it also fostered an environment that prioritized clarity and efficiency.

Opportunities for Go

Rather than being a happy coincidence, the rise of Go as a desired programming language in the field of web development is deeply rooted in the architectural advantages it possesses and the requirements of the modern web. Go's rise to prominence as a desired programming language is not simply a happy coincidence. It is becoming increasingly clear that the advantages of utilizing Go are becoming more apparent as businesses all over the world struggle with the challenge of scaling their digital services.

The performance of Go is typically compared to that of other programming languages such as C and C++. This is consistently cited as one of the most lauded advantages of Go. Go is a language that guarantees type safety and reduces the number of errors that occur during runtime. This is due to the fact that it functions as a statically typed and compiled language. The compiler is responsible for converting the code into machine code during the process of compiling a Go program. This code is then directly executed by the hardware of the system. Direct execution makes it possible to have high throughput and quick startup times, which is an essential feature for web applications that require quick responses. Direct execution also makes it possible to have high throughput. Furthermore, the absence of a virtual machine (like the Java Virtual Machine or the CLR in C#) helps to reduce overhead, which in turn ensures that system resources are utilized to their full potential. This is because the absence of a virtual machine helps to reduce overhead.

This efficiency proves to be of the utmost importance when it comes to cloud deployments, which are characterized by a direct correlation between resource utilization and cost consumption.

There are many different kinds of tasks that are frequently involved in web applications. Two examples of these tasks are the management of multiple user requests and the processing of large datasets. It is possible for these tasks to be completed simultaneously. There is a significant benefit associated with the native support for concurrency that Go provides. This support is achieved through the utilization of goroutines. It is the responsibility of the Go runtime to manage a lightweight thread that is referred to as a goroutine. This type of thread can be created at a cost that is relatively low. In order to prevent the system's resources from being depleted, it is possible to generate thousands or even millions of goroutines. One more characteristic of Go is referred to as channels, and it is this characteristic that makes it possible for goroutines to communicate with one another and synchronize, thereby ensuring that the data is accurate. Applications that run on the web are able to effortlessly manage a large number of tasks that are being carried out simultaneously thanks to the utilization of this advanced concurrency model.

The design philosophy behind Go, on the other hand, places an emphasis on simplicity, despite the fact that it is a powerful language. Go is a programming language that discourages the use of overly complex structures due to its uncluttered and uncluttered syntax. This simplicity translates to codebases that are easy to read and maintain, which is especially beneficial in web development, where projects frequently take years to complete and involve a number of different developers. It is an advantage that cannot be overstated. The dedication of Go to maintaining backward compatibility is demonstrated by the fact that it takes measures to prevent applications from becoming incompatible with language updates. It is essential for projects that will be active for a long period of time to have this kind of predictability because it provides developers with the assurance that their efforts today will not be rendered obsolete by changes in the future.

The standard library that comes with Go is a veritable treasure trove for those who work in the creation of websites. It offers packages that can be used for a wide range of tasks, such as the management of file systems, the creation of web servers, the handling of HTTP requests, and the execution of cryptographic operations at a variety of different levels. Through the utilization of this extensive library, the reliance on third-party packages is decreased, thereby ensuring uniformity and minimizing the potential pitfalls associated with external dependencies. This means that the process of development will be simplified for web developers because a large number of essential tools will be easily accessible. This will be the case because of the fact that this will be the case.

One of the most significant advantages of using Go is that it can be compiled into a single binary, which was mentioned earlier. This is especially true in this day and age, when containerized deployments are becoming increasingly common. The difficulties that are associated with dependency management are significantly reduced as a result of the fact that everything is contained within a single binary. Consequently, this ensures that the environment in which the application was developed is identical to the environment in which it will be deployed, thereby reducing the number of problems that may occur during the deployment process. Furthermore, the cross-compilation feature of Go enables developers to easily compile binaries for a variety of platforms, which further expands the deployment options and possibilities. This is made possible by the fact that Go is a popular programming language.

There are many instances in which the applications of a language in the real world are the most effective way to demonstrate the strengths of the language concerned. The utilization of Go has resulted in the enhancement of the web services offered by a large number of well-known companies and platforms. Docker, the platform that was responsible for bringing about a revolution in containerization, uses Go as its primary programming language. The decision-making process was heavily influenced by the effectiveness of Go as well as its straightforward approach to handling dependencies. A platform that is primarily concerned with isolating application environments must possess these characteristics in order to be truly effective.

Go was utilized in the development of Kubernetes, which is another project that has had a significant impact in the field of cloud orchestration. Within this context, the capabilities of Go to manage large-scale environments that are clustered and to handle distributed systems are demonstrated. Because of the concurrency model that this programming language provides, the streaming giant Twitch is able to handle millions of messages at the same time thanks to the chat services that it provides, which are powered by Go.

Go has been integrated into Uber's microservices ecosystem, which enables the company to successfully manage the enormous amounts of data that are continuously flowing through its platform. This is made possible by Go's exceptional performance and scalability capabilities, which have been incorporated into the ecosystem. Dropbox, a pioneer in the field of cloud storage, migrated certain components of its backend from Python to Go with the intention of taking advantage of the performance advantages offered by Go. For this reason, Dropbox migrated these components from Python to Go.

Not only in terms of its technical merits, but also in terms of the applications it has in the real world, Go's strengths are readily apparent when it comes to web development. When it comes to web development, Go's strengths are readily apparent. Many industry giants have brought attention to the potential and capabilities of the Go programming language in terms of shaping the future of web development as a result of their adoption and advocacy of the language.

Go Toolchain

Go's toolchain is a collection of tools that were developed to make the processes of compiling, linking, testing, and managing Go code easier. It is the source of Go's efficient and powerful programming language. The implementation of this toolchain, which was developed concurrently with the language itself, exemplifies Go's commitment to delivering an integrated and all-encompassing development environment. The toolchain for Go is included in the standard distribution, which ensures that it is consistent and reliable. This is in contrast to the majority of languages, which heavily rely on tools provided by third parties for essential development tasks.

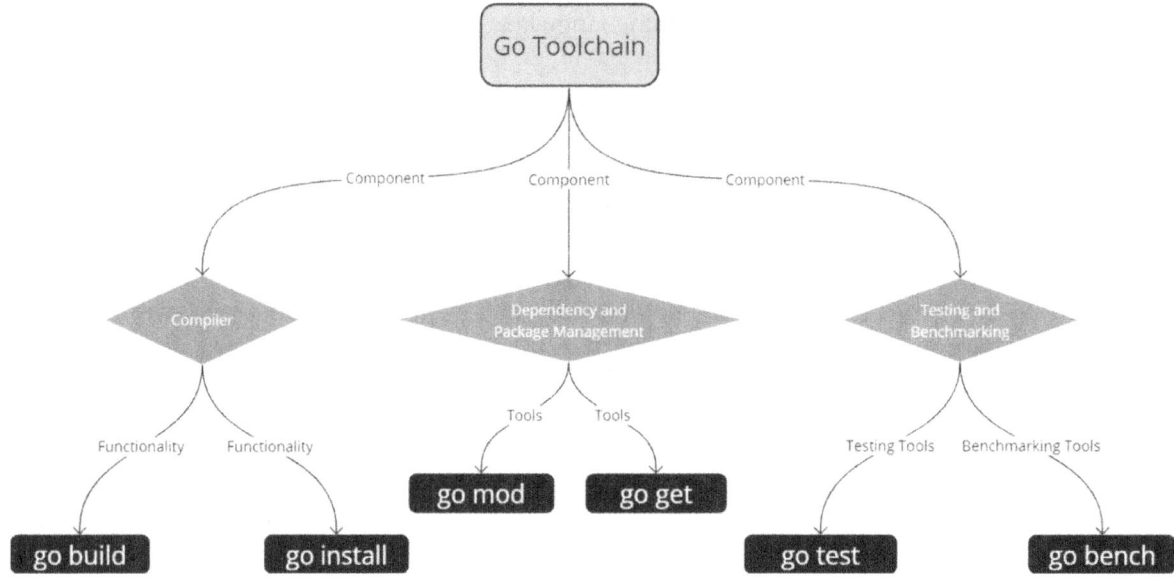

Fig 1.1 Go Toolkit

Compiler

One of the most important tools in the Go toolchain is the compiler, which is responsible for converting Go source code into machine code that can be executed. Accessible through the go build command, the compiler is built with speed in mind, allowing it to generate binaries in a short amount of time. The generated binaries are static by default, which means that they include all dependencies and libraries. This eliminates the typical "dependency hell" that many developers are familiar with. Installing binaries to the $GOPATH/bin directory can be accomplished with the help of the go install command. Because of this separation, developers are able to build locally without increasing the amount of clutter in the global workspace, which promotes clean development practices.

Dependency and Package Management

Dependency management went through a significant transformation when Go 1.11 was released, which was the year that Go Modules were introduced. A workspace that contained all of the Go code and its dependencies was known as the $GOPATH. Prior to this, developers struggled with this workspace. A more decentralized approach was introduced by Go Modules, which enabled code to be stored outside of the $GOPATH directory and introduced versioning. The suite of commands known as go mod is responsible for managing these modules, keeping track of dependencies, and ensuring that builds can be reproduced. In addition to managing the go.mod file, which is responsible for listing all dependencies, it also assists in upgrading or downgrading packages. It retrieves the appropriate versions of libraries.

The go get command makes it possible to retrieve packages from third-party providers in a seamless manner. Through the use of this tool, packages are retrieved from their respective repositories, compiled, and then stored within the workspace. It is a sophisticated solution that combines package retrieval and compilation, which makes it simpler for developers to incorporate external libraries without the need for manual intervention.

Testing and Benchmarking

Quality assurance is an essential part of the development process, and the toolchain that Go provides does not fall short in this regard. When you use the go test command, you will have access to a framework that allows you to write unit tests, run them, and obtain coverage reports. This integrated testing environment guarantees that testing is not an afterthought but rather an essential component of the development cycle. In addition to this, there is a tool called the go bench command that can be used to benchmark Go code. Through its utilization, developers are able to evaluate the performance of their functions, thereby guaranteeing that the code not only functions appropriately but also operates in an effective manner.

While Go's standard toolchain is comprehensive, developers sometimes need to dive deeper or access underlying tools. The go tool command offers this flexibility, providing direct access to tools like the compiler, linker, and trace. For developers seeking granular control or wanting to explore the internals of the Go toolchain, this command is invaluable. This entire toolchain not only simplifies tasks but also ingrains best practices, epitomizing Go's philosophy of simplicity and effectiveness.

Setting up Go on Linux

Installing Go

Setting up Go on Linux is straightforward due to the availability of pre-compiled binary distributions. Before initiating the installation, ensure you have a suitable Linux version. Most modern distributions, be it Ubuntu, CentOS, Fedora, or Debian, support Go.

To start, download the latest Go tarball from the official site. Navigate to Go Downloads and select the appropriate version for Linux.

After downloading, follow these steps:
1. Open your terminal. Navigate to the directory containing the downloaded tarball, typically the Downloads folder.
2. Extract the tarball to /usr/local using the command:

```
sudo tar -C /usr/local -xzf go$VERSION.$OS-$ARCH.tar.gz
```

3. Replace $VERSION, $OS, and $ARCH with the appropriate values from your downloaded file.
4. Adjust the system's PATH to include Go's binaries by editing the profile or bashrc:

```
echo "export PATH=$PATH:/usr/local/go/bin" >> ~/.profile
```

5. Reload the profile using source ~/.profile to ensure the new PATH setting is active.

Configuring Go Workspace

The GOPATH workspace structure was the one that Go utilized in the past. Since the introduction of Go Modules, the implementation of a rigid workspace structure is no longer required. Despite this, it is still possible that organizing your Go projects will be beneficial.

1. Create a directory for your Go projects:

```
mkdir -p ~/go_projects/{bin,src,pkg}
```

2. Set the GOPATH to this directory:

```
echo "export GOPATH=~/go_projects" >> ~/.profile
echo "export PATH=$PATH:$GOPATH/bin" >> ~/.profile
```

3. Again, use source ~/.profile to activate these settings.

Introducing Go Modules

Go Modules, introduced in Go 1.11, is a dependency management system that operates outside the GOPATH. To initiate a new project using Go Modules:

1. Navigate to your project directory.
2. Initialize a new module with:

```
go mod init <module-name>
```

3. This command creates a go.mod file which tracks your project's dependencies.

Setting up Tools and Libraries

For web development, certain libraries and tools enhance the Go experience. Given below is a brief setup:

1. Gorilla Mux - A versatile router and dispatcher:

go get -u github.com/gorilla/mux

2. GORM - An ORM library for Go:

go get -u gorm.io/gorm

3. GoDotEnv - Manage environment variables:

go get -u github.com/joho/godotenv

4. Fresh - A tool for auto-reloading your web applications during development:

go get github.com/pilu/fresh

When you use these packages in your code and build your application, they will be automatically added to the go.mod file. This is something you should keep in mind when working with Go Modules.

IDE and Code Editors

Consider utilizing an Integrated Development Environment (IDE) or a text editor that is specifically designed for Go in order to improve the quality of your coding experience. Among the preferred options are:
1. A comprehensive Go development experience is made available by Visual Studio Code (VS Code) when the Go extension is installed. This extension includes features such as code navigation, IntelliSense, and debugging.
2. As a dedicated Go integrated development environment (IDE), GoLand by JetBrains offers powerful coding, testing, and debugging features.

To set up VS Code, download the .deb or .rpm package from the official site and install it. After launching VS Code, search for the Go extension by Google and install it.

With Go installed, the workspace configured, the necessary libraries downloaded, and a code editor installed, you're ready to dive deep into web development with Go. The Linux environment is particularly well-suited for the development of Go because it provides both flexibility and power. Just the tip of the iceberg is represented by the tools and libraries that have been mentioned here. Despite the fact that the initial setup may appear to be extensive, it is actually a one-time effort that paves the way for a coding journey that is both smooth and productive.

net/http Package
net/http Overview
Go's net/http package sits at the core of its web development capabilities. As a part of the standard library, this package offers a plethora of functionalities, ranging from the basics of setting up a server and handling HTTP requests, to more intricate aspects like cookies, redirects, and file uploads. The true beauty of net/http lies in its simplicity, abstracting away the complexities of the HTTP protocol while allowing developers to focus on the application logic.

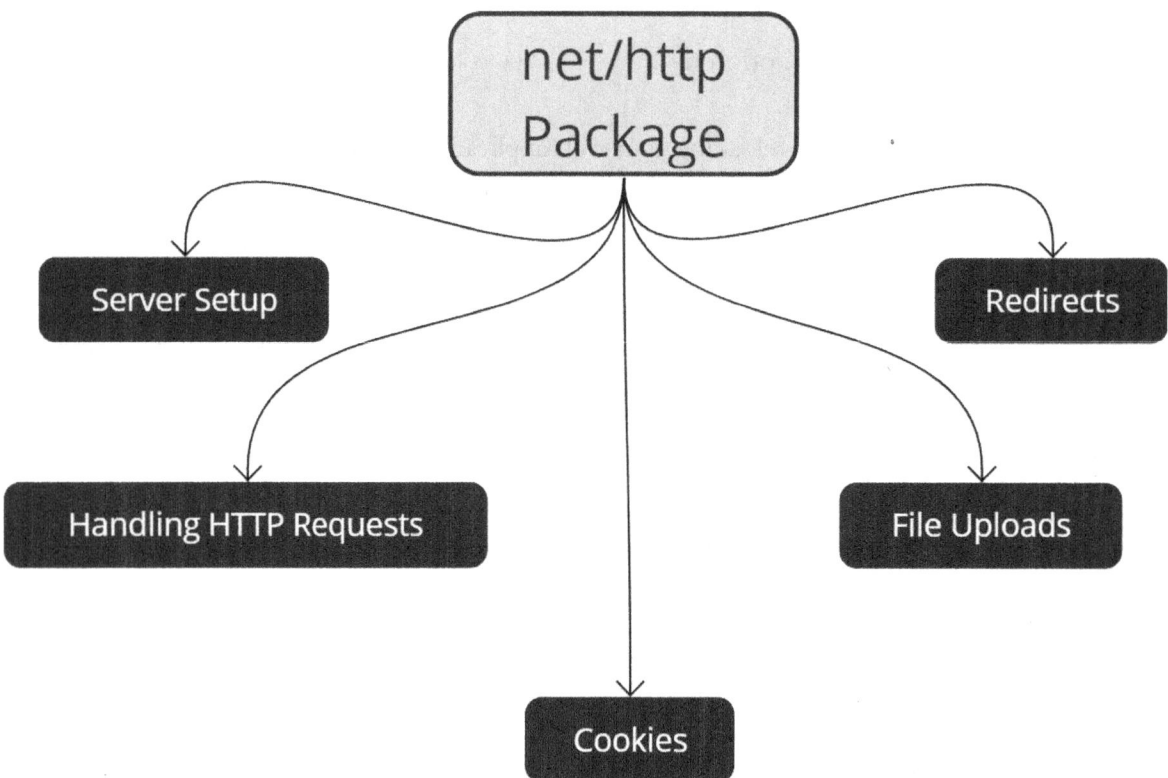

Fig 1.2 Overview of net/http Package

HTTP Servers and Clients
The dual capability of net/http to both function as an HTTP client and to set up HTTP servers

is the core competency of this programming language. Using the ListenAndServe function, developers are able to quickly start a server. This function begins listening on a particular port for incoming HTTP requests and begins listening for them. When it comes to server configuration, one of Go's most notable characteristics is its ease of use, which enables rapid development and deployment. To facilitate outbound requests to other servers on the web, the package provides developers with functions such as Get and Post, amongst others, which are available on the client side of the application. Go's dedication to delivering a comprehensive web development experience is highlighted by the fact that it incorporates both client and server functionality into a single package.

Handlers and HandlerFuncs

The ability to comprehend handlers is an essential component of working with net/http software. A handler is any object that adheres to the http.Handler interface in the context of Go. This interface requires a method with the signature ServeHTTP(http.ResponseWriter, *http.Request). Go's handlers are required to have this signature. Developers are able to create custom handlers that are tailored to the specific requirements of their application thanks to this design, which allows for a great deal of flexibility. The *http.Request class is responsible for encapsulating all of the information regarding the incoming request, while the http.ResponseWriter class plays an important role in the process of sending responses back to the client. The Go programming language provides a convenient adapter called http.HandlerFunc, which enables regular functions to function as HTTP handlers. This simplifies the process of implementing handlers, making the experience more streamlined.

Routing Requests

While the basic server creation is straightforward, real-world applications often demand intricate routing mechanisms. Though net/http doesn't provide an extensive router akin to some third-party packages, it offers a multiplexer called http.ServeMux. This multiplexer can route requests based on their URL patterns to specific handlers. For complex applications with dynamic URL patterns, developers often turn to third-party routers like Gorilla Mux. However, for simpler applications, http.ServeMux suffices.

Data Request and Response

Deep interactions with incoming requests and crafting responses form a significant part of web development. The net/http package provides comprehensive tools for this. For example, the http.Request type contains methods to parse query parameters, extract form data, and read the request body. On the response side, http.ResponseWriter facilitates setting headers, writing response data, and configuring status codes.

Using net/http

Now, shifting focus to integrating net/http into the development environment. As net/http is part of Go's standard library, there's no separate installation process like third-party packages. Once Go is set up on your machine, the net/http package is ready for use.

To use it in your Go application:
- At the beginning of your Go file, add the import statement: import "net/http".
- Post-import, you can leverage any functionality from the net/http package. Whether it's starting a server with http.ListenAndServe or crafting an HTTP client request using http.Get.
- Dive into the extensive documentation available on the official Go website or access it directly through the godoc command. This will provide insights into the plethora of functionalities net/http offers.

The net/http package in Go is not merely a library; rather, it is a gateway to the development of sophisticated web applications in the Go programming language. Because of its emphasis on simplicity and functionality, it gives developers the ability to construct and manage web servers, handle requests and responses with dexterity, and create routing mechanisms that can accommodate the requirements of both straightforward and intricate applications. As a result, it exemplifies Go's philosophy of making powerful web development accessible and manageable, which is one of the reasons why Go is becoming an increasingly popular choice for web development.

Introducing Bookstore Web Application

The world of books is vast, encompassing millennia of human knowledge and creativity. In this digital age, accessing books has transformed from physical visits to online searches and purchases. Our project, the "Bookstore Web Application," aims to mirror this digital transformation. The application will serve as an online platform where users can browse, search, review, and purchase books. While it might seem like just another web application, building it from scratch will immerse you in a myriad of web development concepts, tools, and best practices, all centered around the Go programming language.

Our Bookstore application will not be a mere static site. It will be interactive, dynamic, and user-centric. Some of the core features will include:
- User Authentication: Users will register, log in, and maintain profiles, ensuring personalized experiences.
- Book Listings: An extensive catalog displaying books with their cover images, descriptions, authors, and pricing.
- Search and Filter: A robust search mechanism to pinpoint specific books, supplemented with filters like genres, authors, and ratings.
- Shopping Cart: Users can add books to their cart, view cart contents, and proceed to purchase.

- Reviews and Ratings: Post-purchase, users can leave reviews and ratings, fostering a community-driven recommendation system.
- Admin Dashboard: A separate interface for administrators to manage book listings, track sales, and interact with user feedback.

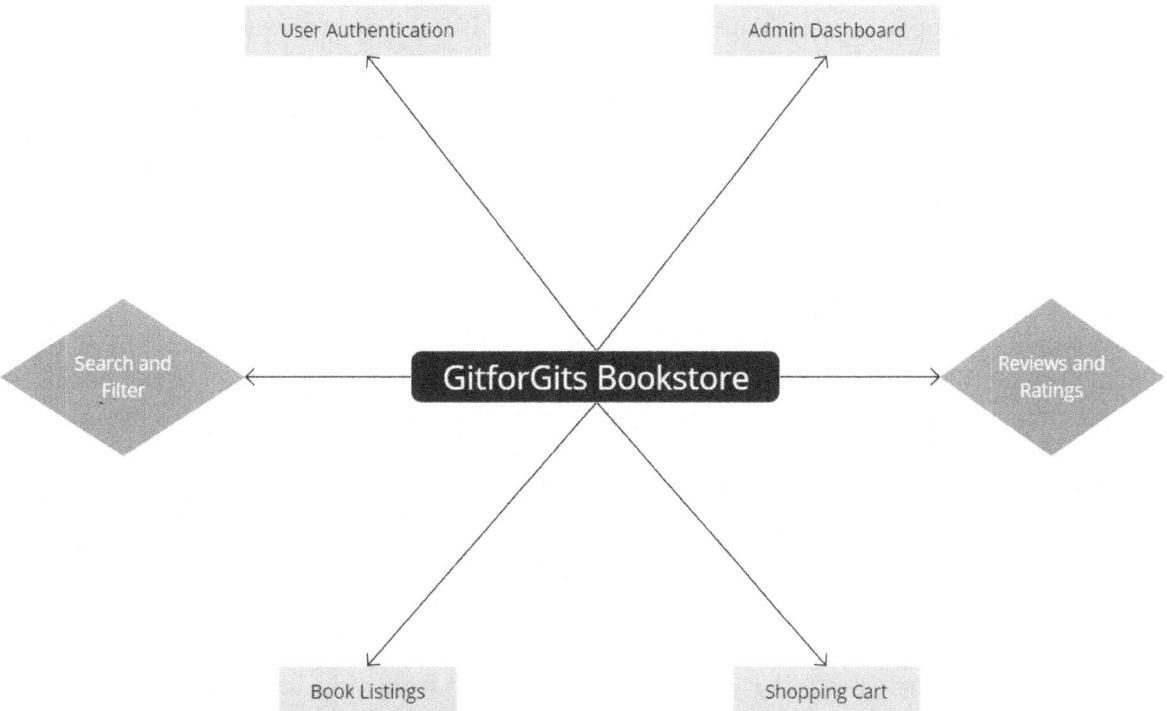

Fig 1.3 Functionalities of GitforGits Bookstore Application

Building the Bookstore application is not just about the end product; it's the journey that counts.

Following is what you will learn in the entire building of bookstore web application:
- Understanding how Go structures web applications, from organizing files and folders to modularizing code for scalability.
- Engaging with databases to store and retrieve data, using Go's database packages and third-party ORMs. You will grasp CRUD operations, migrations, and advanced querying.
- Handling user sessions, cookies, and ensuring data persistence across interactions.
- Leveraging Go's templating engine to create dynamic web pages that change based on data.
- Processing user input, validation, and ensuring data integrity.
- Implementing middleware for tasks like logging, authentication, and error handling.

Understanding the depth of HTTP handlers in routing requests.
- Using Go's concurrency model to handle simultaneous user requests efficiently.
- Writing tests for the application, debugging issues, and ensuring code reliability.
- Taking the application live, understanding cloud hosting, containerization, and ensuring the application scales with user demand.

The Bookstore application isn't just another project; it's a representation of real-world web applications that millions interact with daily. By building it, you not only understand the "how" but also the "why" behind design decisions, tool choices, and architectural considerations. Each feature of the Bookstore is carefully chosen to introduce a new concept or deepen understanding of an existing one. You aren't just learning Go web development in isolation; you're understanding it in the context of the broader web development landscape.

Go RESTful Services

It is possible to have a comprehensive understanding of RESTful services in Go by looking at them through the lens of REST's fundamental principles and the distinctive capabilities of the Go programming language. An architectural style that was conceived of by Dr. Roy Fielding is known as REST, which is an acronym that stands for "Representational State Transfer." In contrast to a standard, it is a set of guidelines for the development of web services that are scalable and easy to maintain. These guidelines are typically implemented using HTTP.

Key Principles of REST

The REST methodology is based on a number of fundamental principles. It places an emphasis on statelessness, which means that every request that is sent from a client to a server must contain all of the information that is required for the server to process it, without relying on any session state that has been stored. This approach is consistent with the design of Go, which has a preference for straightforwardness and simplicity. The client-server architecture that is used in REST serves to encourage a separation of concerns. The client is responsible for the user interface and experience, while the server is in charge of the data and the operations that take place on the back end. When it comes to managing the various components of an application, this separation is analogous to the modular approach that Go takes.

Cacheability is another principle, which states that RESTful responses should be explicitly marked as cacheable or non-cacheable. This results in improved performance, which is a goal that Go also strives to achieve due to the fact that it is compiled and efficient. Go's ability to create scalable and maintainable systems is reminiscent of the layered system that is used in REST. In this system, a client interacts with an end server or intermediaries without having to differentiate between them. The uniform interface principle simplifies the architecture by making interactions predictable and standardized. This is similar to the straightforward syntax of Go as well as its approach to interfaces and methods.

Implementing RESTful Services with Go

Its standard library, in particular the net/http package, contributes significantly to the ease with which RESTful services can be developed. It is common practice for developers to make use of the http.HandleFunc() method or third-party routers in order to define endpoints and associate HTTP methods such as GET, POST, PUT, and DELETE with these endpoints. This package gives developers the ability to do so. For the purpose of identifying resources in REST, URIs are utilized, and the powerful URL parsing capabilities of Go come in handy for this purpose.

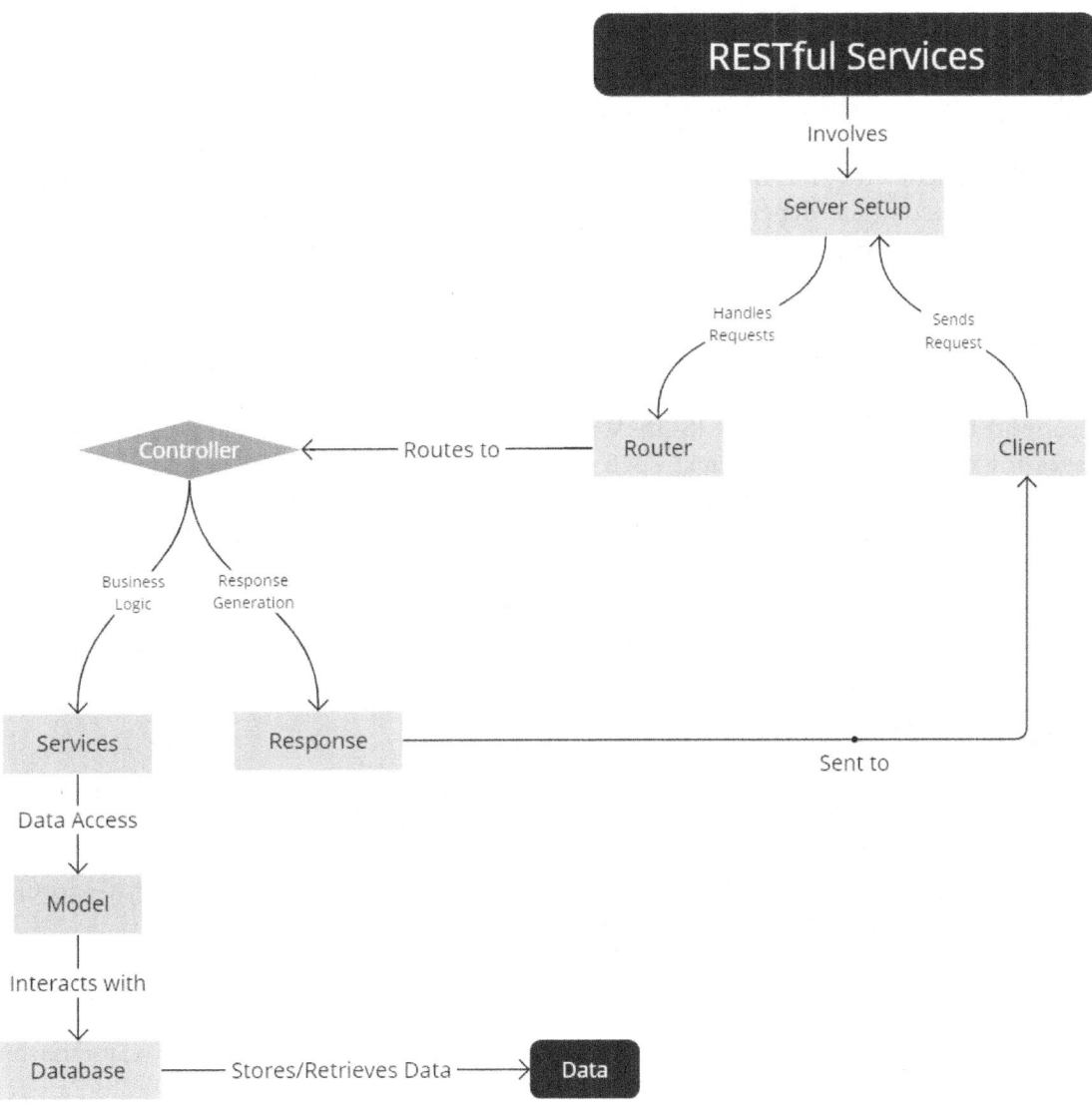

Fig 1.4 Implementing RESTful Services in Go

Each request that is sent to a Go server should carry all of the necessary data because REST is a stateless protocol. Go is an excellent option for RESTful services that require format flexibility in communication because of its ability to handle HTTP requests and responses, as well as its support for JSON and XML through packages such as encoding/json. Additionally, RESTful services rely heavily on Go's error handling, which lets developers supply useful error messages and suitable HTTP status codes. It is a good fit between the explicit error handling of Go and the requirement that REST has for clear communication of problems.

Go's Advantage in RESTful Development

There are a number of characteristics of Go that make it an excellent choice for the development of RESTful services. When it comes to high-traffic services, its performance as a compiled language is absolutely essential. Native support for concurrency in Go makes it possible to handle multiple simultaneous requests in an efficient manner, which is a scenario that frequently occurs in RESTful services. The dependability on external packages is decreased as a result of the robustness of the standard library. Strong typing and support for JSON are two features that guarantee the integrity of data in Go.

Additionally, the language's support for middleware enables additional functionalities such as logging and authentication.The security of Go's RESTful services is of the utmost importance. Go's support for HTTPS, the use of JSON Web Tokens for authentication, and the utilization of packages for the prevention of attacks such as CSRF are all options that developers can take advantage of. The approach that Go takes to sanitizing and validating inputs is absolutely necessary in order to protect against threats such as SQL injection. As developers work their way through the process of developing the Bookstore application, they will make use of the features that Go offers in order to create RESTful routes. This will ensure that books are not only listed, but also interacted with, in accordance with the most effective principles of web service design.

Building my First Web Server

Exciting is the feeling that comes with beginning the process of developing a web server, particularly one that will eventually develop into a comprehensive application for BookStore. In the beginning, it is all about establishing a foundation, gaining an understanding of the complexities, and achieving that "Hello, World!" moment – or, in our case, "Hello GitforGits BookStore!"

Initializing Project

Every great application starts with a structured workspace. Before diving into code, establish a directory for the BookStore project. Using your terminal or command line:

mkdir gitforgits-bookstore

```
cd gitforgits-bookstore
```

Next, initialize a Go module to manage dependencies:

```
go mod init gitforgits-bookstore
```

This command creates a go.mod file, which will list and manage all project dependencies as we add them.

Crafting Basic Server

As soon as the workspace is prepared, we shall get started by constructing a fundamental server.

To begin, create a new file and give it the name main.proceed to the directory of the project. Within this file, the primary logic of the server will be stored.

Within main.go, start by importing the necessary packages:

```go
package main

import (
        "fmt"
        "net/http"
)
```

The net/http package provides functionalities for building HTTP servers and clients, while fmt will be used for formatting our output.

Now, define the main function and set up the server:

```go
func main() {
        http.HandleFunc("/", homeHandler)
        http.ListenAndServe(":8080", nil)
}
```

In the following, two crucial steps are taken:
1. http.HandleFunc("/", homeHandler): This line maps the root URL ("/") to a function named homeHandler, which we'll define shortly.

2. http.ListenAndServe(":8080", nil): This instructs the application to start an HTTP server on port 8080.

Next, we shall define the homeHandler function:

```
func homeHandler(w http.ResponseWriter, r *http.Request) {
    fmt.Fprintf(w, "Hello GitforGits BookStore!")
}
```

This function takes in two parameters: http.ResponseWriter and *http.Request. The http.ResponseWriter is an interface that allows sending a response back to the client, while *http.Request provides information about the incoming request.

Running the Server

To experience the magic of the first server, navigate to the project directory in your terminal and run:

```
go run main.go
```

If everything goes as planned, the server starts listening on port 8080. By visiting http://localhost:8080 in a web browser, the greeting "Hello GitforGits BookStore!" should warmly welcome you.

Despite the fact that this initial server might appear to be straightforward, it will serve as the foundation upon which the entire BookStore application will be constructed. A directory structure has been established, the fundamental flow of a Go-based server has been comprehended, and we have become acquainted with fundamental concepts such as handlers. The subsequent chapters and sections will delve deeper, introducing dynamic content rendering, intricate routing, and database connections. These will be built upon the foundation that has been laid.

Summary

In this chapter, we started the fundamental process of building a Go web server for our project, which is called "GitforGits BookStore." The readers were educated on the significance of creating a dedicated directory and initializing a Go module for efficient dependency management, beginning with the establishment of an organized workspace. This was done in order to ensure that everyone was on the same page. As a result of taking this first step, it ensures that the development environment is clean and well-structured, which makes the process of adding dependencies and managing them more efficient as the project grows.

Through an examination of the code, the chapter provided an explanation of the fundamental operations involved in establishing a basic HTTP server by utilizing the net/http package in Go. This chapter provided readers with an introduction to the http.HandleFunc function, which is an important tool that links particular URLs with the handler functions that correspond to them. By acquiring this foundational knowledge, you are laying the groundwork for more complex routing and request handling in later stages of the project. In addition, the http.ListenAndServe function was presented, which gave an example of how Go applications can be instructed to launch an HTTP server on a particular port, ready to deal with requests from clients that are coming in.

By demonstrating how handler functions manage incoming web requests and generate appropriate responses, the chapter also brought attention to the significance of handler functions and the organization of these functions. The homeHandler function served as an example of how to make use of the http.ResponseWriter and *http.Request parameters. Both the transmission of data to clients and the retrieval of information about incoming requests are made possible by these essential elements for developers. The readers were able to realize the results of their efforts by executing the server with the go run command and observing the greeting message "Hello GitforGits BookStore!" on their web browser. This resulted in the transformation of abstract knowledge into concrete outcomes.

Throughout the entirety of this chapter, the primary focus was placed on the construction of a fundamental server; however, the goal was to acquire an understanding of the fundamental principles of web development using Go. During the practice of the development of the project, the skills and concepts that have been presented will be reviewed, elaborated upon, and incorporated into more intricate functionalities. This will ensure that the learning experience is both comprehensive and engaging.

Chapter 2: Structuring Go Web Application

Explore Go Modules

The next evolutionary step in dependency management for the Go programming language is represented by modules. Prior to the introduction of modules, the Go ecosystem was dependent on the GOPATH workspace, which was a place where all source codes and the dependencies that accompany them coexisted. In spite of the fact that it was functional, this structure presented difficulties in terms of versioning and project isolation. Go Modules, which were first introduced in Go version 1.11, emerged as a solution to these challenges. They revolutionized the way dependencies are handled, making it simpler, more intuitive, and detached from the GOPATH.

Essence of Go Modules

At its core, a Go module is a collection of Go packages stored in a file tree with a go.mod file at the root. This file is the module's manifest, detailing its module path, which is its import path prefix, and its dependency requirements.

Modules offer several compelling advantages:
- Modules inherently support versioning. Developers can specify which version of a dependency they wish to use, and Go ensures that that exact version is employed consistently across builds.
- With modules, projects are isolated. Gone are the days of the monolithic GOPATH. Developers can now work on multiple projects with differing dependencies without conflict.
- The go.sum file, accompanying the go.mod file, ensures that the modules used are precisely what the developer expects. It contains cryptographic checksums of module content, providing an added layer of security and consistency.
- Modules can be located anywhere, not just in GOPATH or version control systems. They can reside on local file systems, network servers, or even be fetched via proxy servers.

Transitioning to Modules

The introduction of modules in Go marks a significant shift from the traditional GOPATH-based workflow, offering a more streamlined and intuitive approach to dependency management. This transition is especially beneficial for developers looking to modernize their workflow, simplify package management, and improve the reproducibility of builds.

For developers starting new projects, adopting modules is incredibly straightforward. The initiation of a new module begins with a simple command:

go mod init <module-name>

This command creates a new go.mod file in the project directory. This file is key to modules, as it tracks the project's dependencies. The <module-name> is typically the repository location where your module will be published, but it can be any string for internal or unpublished modules.

The transition to modules is not just limited to new projects. Existing codebases can also adapt to this new system with minimal friction. When Go tools like go build or go test are executed inside a project that doesn't contain a go.mod file and is outside the GOPATH, Go automatically begins the migration process. This automated migration is a cornerstone feature, aimed at reducing the complexities traditionally associated with dependency management. During this migration, Go analyzes the existing code and dependencies, creating a go.mod file along with a go.sum file. The go.sum file plays a crucial role in ensuring the integrity of the dependencies by storing their expected cryptographic checksums.

Dependency Management with Modules

The development of applications relies heavily on effective dependency management, and this is where Go Modules, a built-in dependency management tool, shines. Go Modules provides a streamlined and intuitive approach to managing project dependencies, which is essential for the development of applications.

It is a testament to Go's commitment to simplicity and efficiency that the process of adding a new dependency in a Go project using Modules is remarkably straightforward. When a developer imports a package that is not already included in the project, the build command (go build or go test) causes Go to automatically locate, download, and add that dependency to the go.mod file. This occurs when the build command is executed. After that, this file functions as a manifest, providing information about the particular versions of each dependency that is utilized in the project. This automated addition helps to reduce the amount of manual oversight that is required and guarantees that all necessary dependencies are declared explicitly.

In scenarios where developers need to fetch a specific version of a module, the go get command becomes indispensable:

go get <module-path>@<version>

This command allows precise control over the versions of dependencies being used. For instance, if a particular version of a library is known to work best with the project, it can be explicitly specified. This command updates the go.mod file to reflect the specified version, ensuring consistency across different development environments.

go mod tidy

This powerful command cleans up the go.mod and the accompanying go.sum file, which maintains a checksum for each dependency. It removes references to dependencies no longer used in the project, making the go.mod file a true reflection of the project's current state.

Understanding Module Proxies

An intermediary between Go projects and source repositories is the primary function of a module proxy in Go. This role is performed by the module proxy. If a Go project makes a request for a module, the proxy will retrieve and store the module from its source, which could be a website such as GitHub. Subsequent requests for the same module are served from the cache of the proxy, which significantly reduces the amount of time required to retrieve the module.

Using a module proxy allows for faster module retrieval, which is one of the most significant advantages of using this type of proxy. The fact that modules are cached eliminates the need to repeatedly download the same module (across a variety of projects or builds), which results in a reduction in the amount of time required for the build process. When it comes to larger projects, such as the GitforGits Bookstore, where there may be multiple dependencies involved, this is especially helpful.

Enhanced dependability is yet another significant advantage that comes with utilizing a module proxy. It is common practice for Go projects to host their dependencies on a variety of source control systems located all over the internet. For the purpose of providing stability and continuity, a module proxy ensures that the cached version will continue to be accessible even in the event that the original source is removed or becomes unavailable.

Understanding and leveraging the power of module proxies is a critical aspect of efficient and secure software development for developers working on Go projects such as the GitforGits Bookstore. Within the modern workflow for Go development, module proxies are an essential tool that must be utilized, regardless of whether the default Go proxy is utilized or a custom proxy is established.

Standard Go Directory Structure

Go, in contrast to a number of other programming languages, does not strictly enforce a particular directory structure. On the other hand, over the course of many years, the community has come to a consensus on a number of conventions that improve the readability of code, make tooling easier, and make maintenance simpler. The GOPATH workspace, which was a directory where all Go projects were stored, was the primary resource for Go developers prior to the introduction of modules. There were three primary subdirectories in this workspace: src, which contained source files; pkg, which contained package objects; and bin, which contained compiled binaries. Afterwards, individual projects would be stored in the directories that were named after their domains, which would be contained within the src directory.

Take, for instance, the following: src/github.com/gitforgits/bookstore.

Using modules, the GOPATH workspace became less rigid, which was a significant improvement. It became possible for projects to be located outside of the GOPATH, and the structure of the directory became more adaptable. Nevertheless, there are a few conventions that continue to exist:
- Cmd Directory: Contains application commands. Every application should reside in its directory named after the application, and there should be one main file per application directory.
- Pkg Directory: Houses libraries and packages used in multiple applications across a project but not externally.
- Api Directory: Used for API definitions and protocol files.
- Web or Ui Directory: Contains web assets, templates, and frontend-related content.
- Scripts Directory: Houses scripts used for various purposes, like building or deployment.

Designing Directory Structure

Starting with a directory structure that is well-organized is an essential step in the process of developing a comprehensive application such as the GitforGits Bookstore. In addition to facilitating better management and understanding of the code, this structure is also aligned with the best practices of Go, which makes it simpler for any developer to navigate the project and contribute to it.

Root Directory Essentials

The root directory of GitforGits Bookstore will host several critical files:
- README.md: Provides documentation and an overview of the project.
- LICENSE: Contains licensing information.
- go.mod and go.sum: Facilitate module management, signaling Go's modular approach.

Directory Breakdown

1. Cmd Directory: This will house the applications within our project. For simplicity, we shall assume the primary application is the server itself:
   - cmd/server: Contains the main function that initiates our server. The entry point of our web application.

2. Pkg Directory: A place for our libraries and packages. The shared logic and components which might not be exclusive to the web application, potentially used in future command-line tools or other applications:
   - pkg/models: Essential data structures like book.go or user.go.
   - pkg/utils: Utility functions such as auth.go for authentication mechanisms or helpers.go for various helper functions.

3. Api Directory: Given the importance of clear API definitions in modern web apps:
   - api/definitions: Potential OpenAPI or gRPC definitions, detailing the contract

our server provides.

4. Web Directory: All things front-end:
   - web/static: Static assets, including CSS, JS, images, or even third-party libraries.
   - web/templates: Go HTML templates, allowing dynamic content rendering.

5. Internal Directory: Code meant exclusively for this application and not for external use.
   - internal/handlers: HTTP handlers, like bookHandler.go for serving book-related requests or userHandler.go for user operations.
   - internal/middleware: Essential middleware functions for tasks like logging, CORS, or authentication.
   - internal/config: Configuration-related logic, maybe config.go which might fetch and parse configuration details.

6. Scripts Directory: Any script aiding development, deployment, or other operations:
   - scripts/deploy.sh: A potential script to handle deployment.
   - scripts/test.sh: Running tests or linters across the project.

7. Database Directory: For database-related files and scripts.
   - database/migrations: SQL scripts or other migration tools to ensure database structure consistency.
   - database/seeds: Scripts or data files that seed initial data into the database.

8. Docs Directory: For comprehensive documentation, other than the main README.
   - docs/setup.md: Setup and installation instructions.
   - docs/api.md: API endpoints, request-response examples, and other API-related documentation.

Creating the Directory Structure

To set up this structure, simple terminal commands can be used:

```
mkdir gitforgits-bookstore && cd gitforgits-bookstore
mkdir cmd pkg api web internal scripts database docs
mkdir cmd/server pkg/models pkg/utils api/definitions web/static web/templates
internal/handlers internal/middleware internal/config database/migrations database/seeds
touch go.mod README.md LICENSE
```

The directory structure outlined is both conventional, adhering to Go best practices, and tailored, meeting the specific needs of the GitforGits Bookstore Web App. The aim is to ensure that any developer, familiar with Go or new to the project, can quickly understand the application's layout and know precisely where to look for specific functionalities. As we progress through the subsequent chapters and delve deeper into the intricacies of web application development using Go, this structure will be our guiding map, ensuring that every piece of code finds its logical home.

Package Management and Vendoring

Regardless of the programming environment, packages or libraries are used to enhance the capabilities of the core language. This enables developers to make use of code that has already been written. The process of importing, managing, and making use of these external packages in a methodical fashion is the essence of what is known as package management. In the Go programming language, this refers to the process by which these external pieces of code are added, updated, or removed in order to guarantee a smooth integration with the primary application.

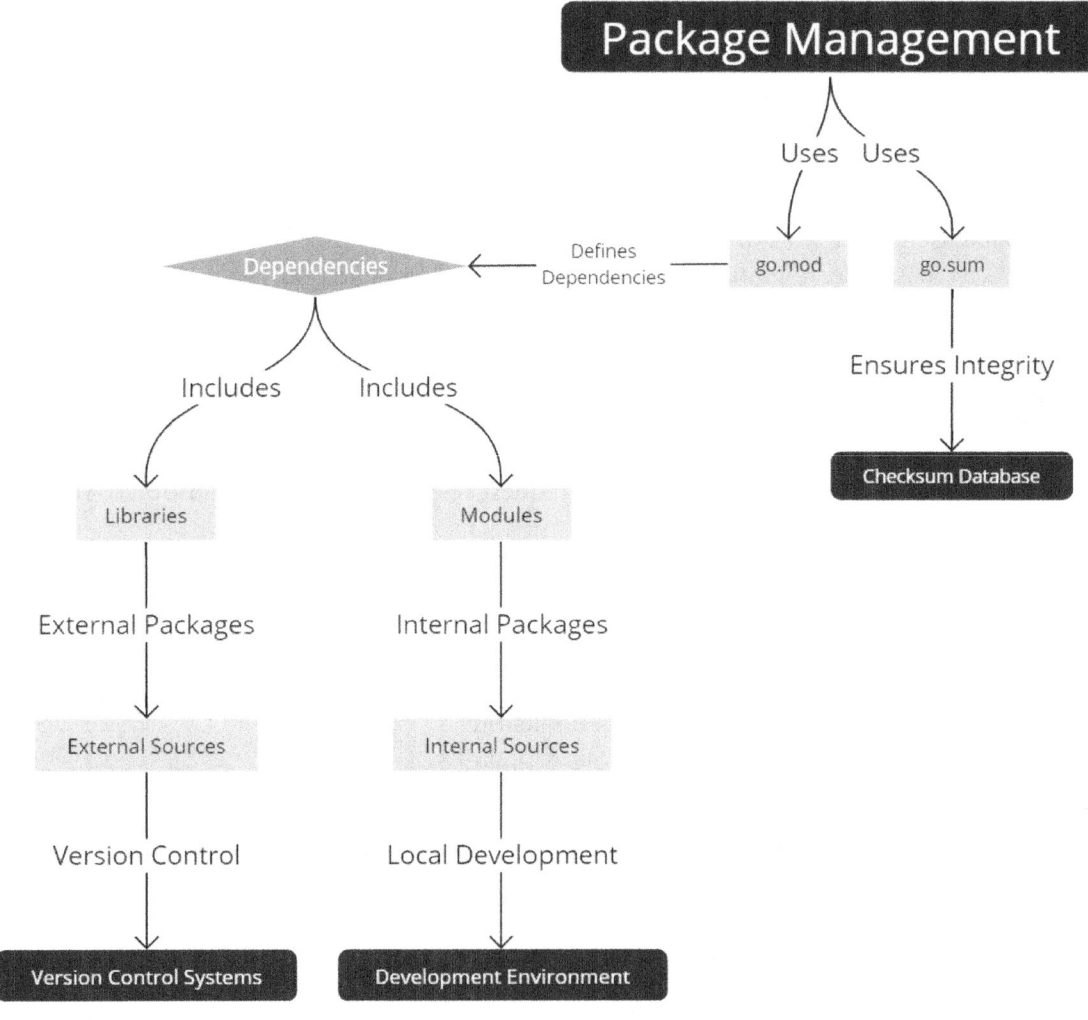

Fig 2.1 Package Management in Go

Why Package Management Matters?

When it comes to the development of modern software, package management is an essential component. It is able to ensure consistency across all developer environments, isolate project dependencies, and enable reproducible builds thanks to its capabilities. These capabilities provide the essential foundations for software projects that are scalable and maintainable throughout their lifetime.

Consistency Across Environments

Package managers allow all developers working on a project to use precisely the same versions of external libraries and modules. This consistency eliminates bugs and errors that can emerge when some engineers use updated packages while others use older legacy versions. Package managers install dependencies in a contained project context, ensuring everyone harmonizes around a uniform set of packages.

Isolation from Global State

Package managers enable dependency isolation by installing packages in an encapsulated project context rather than globally. This allows distinctly defining a project's dependencies, separate from any packages installed globally on the system. Isolation enhances portability and enables a project to function uniformly across different target environments.

Reproducible and Reliable Builds

By using a fixed and consistent set of dependency versions during builds, package managers enable reliably reproducible builds. Automated builds will integrate the exact same dependencies defined in the project manifest file. This reproducibility provides tremendous confidence during continuous delivery pipelines. Build artifacts can be identically recreated across environments. Reproducible builds also aid tremendously with debugging by eliminating uncertainty around underlying packages.

Need of Vendoring

In the Go programming language, the process of copying all of your external dependencies into your project directory is referred to as "vendoring." Prior to the introduction of Go Modules, the recommended method for achieving reproducible builds was to use vendoring. When using vendoring, the external packages that are associated with the project are typically kept in a directory within the project that is labelled /vendor. The packages in the /vendor directory are given higher priority by Go during the application's construction process than those in the global GOPATH directory.

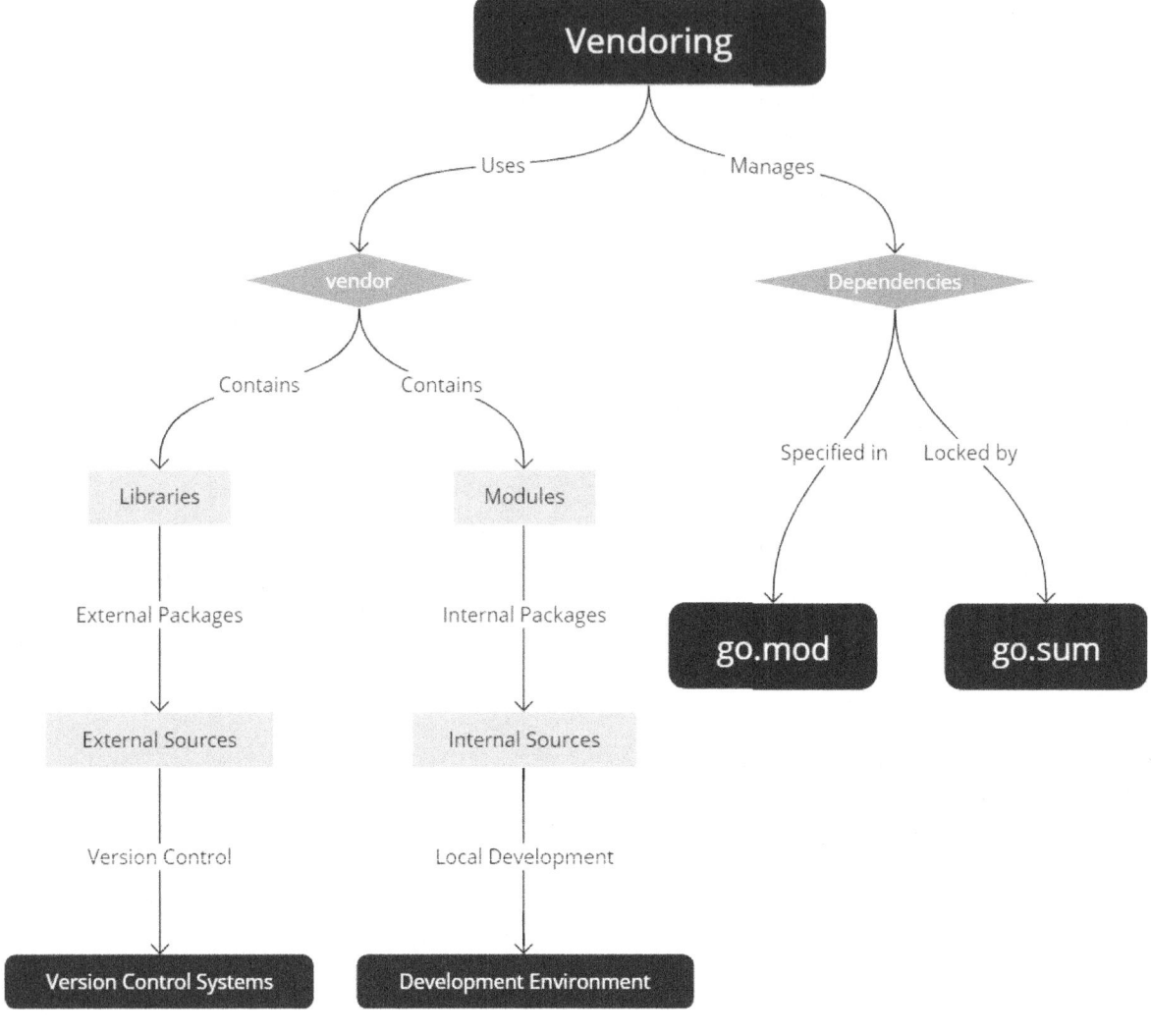

Fig 2.2 Vendoring in Go

Benefits of Vendoring
- Your project is isolated from system-wide packages, ensuring that updates or removals in the global space don't affect your project.
- Since all dependencies are local, you can build your project without internet access.
- Your dependencies won't change unless you explicitly decide to update them, leading to reproducible builds.

Traditional vendoring has been replaced by a new approach within the Go community. An integrated mechanism for dependency management is provided by Go Modules, which eliminates the requirement for a vendor directory in an explicit manner. Go Modules, on the other hand, offer an opt-in vendoring mode that allows the /vendor directory to be populated by the go mod vendor command. This mode is designed for those individuals who continue to favor vendoring due to the benefits it offers.

Implementing Package Management

Initiating Go Modules

If not done already, you then initiate Go Modules for the project. This creates the go.mod and go.sum files, tracking the project's dependencies.

```
go mod init gitforgits-bookstore
```

Adding Dependencies

As you code and import new packages, Go will automatically add them to the go.mod file. For manual addition:

```
go get <package-name>@<version>
```

This fetches the desired package version and adds it to the go.mod file.

Updating and Removing

Go makes it easy to update packages to newer versions or remove unused ones. To update:

```
go get -u <package-name>
```

To remove unused packages:

```
go mod tidy
```

Vendoring with Go Modules

When it comes to those who are inclined towards vendoring, even with Go Modules in place, the process is straightforward. When you have finished managing your dependencies, simply run:

```
go mod vendor
```

This populates the /vendor directory with the project's dependencies, ensuring builds use these vendored packages.

Maintaining and Reviewing

Periodically, it's wise to review and update the dependencies. This not only fetches updates with potential new features but also ensures security by patching any vulnerabilities in the used packages.

Go's dependency management landscape has become more streamlined and efficient, particularly since the introduction of modules. This is especially true in that context. For the GitforGits Bookstore Web App, the focus continues to be on ensuring consistency, reproducibility, and isolation. This is true regardless of whether pure Go Modules are selected or whether the app is integrated with vendoring.

Model-View-Controller (MVC) in Go

Understanding MVC

The MVC paradigm is an architectural pattern that has stood the test of time, becoming a cornerstone for web applications across numerous programming languages. Its essence lies in compartmentalizing an application into three interconnected components:

1. Model: Represents the data structure and business logic. In essence, the model is the backbone, housing the rules, data, and the logic to update or process this data.
2. View: Focuses on the presentation layer. It's what the end-users interact with - the UI. Views display data from the model to the user and send user commands to the controller.
3. Controller: Acts as an intermediary between the Model and View. It takes user input from the view, processes it (with potential updates to the model), and returns the output display to the view.

While Go isn't strictly an MVC framework like Ruby on Rails for Ruby or Django for Python, its flexibility allows developers to architect web applications in the MVC style. The Go standard library, especially the net/http package, combined with several third-party packages, offers a comprehensive toolkit to implement an MVC pattern.

Benefits of MVC

- Separation of Concerns: By decoupling data handling, user interface, and control flow, the MVC pattern ensures that each component of the GitforGits Bookstore remains independent. This separation is conducive to parallel development, unit testing, and scalability.
- Modularity: As the GitforGits Bookstore grows, adding features or making changes becomes less daunting. If, for instance, the way books are fetched changes, modifications are localized to the Model, without altering the View or Controller.
- Reusability: Components, especially views and models, can be reused across different parts of the application. For example, a book model can be used in various contexts – search, recommendations, user history – without duplication.

Maintenance: A well-structured MVC application simplifies maintenance. With clear boundaries between components, locating issues, updating features, or refactoring becomes more straightforward.

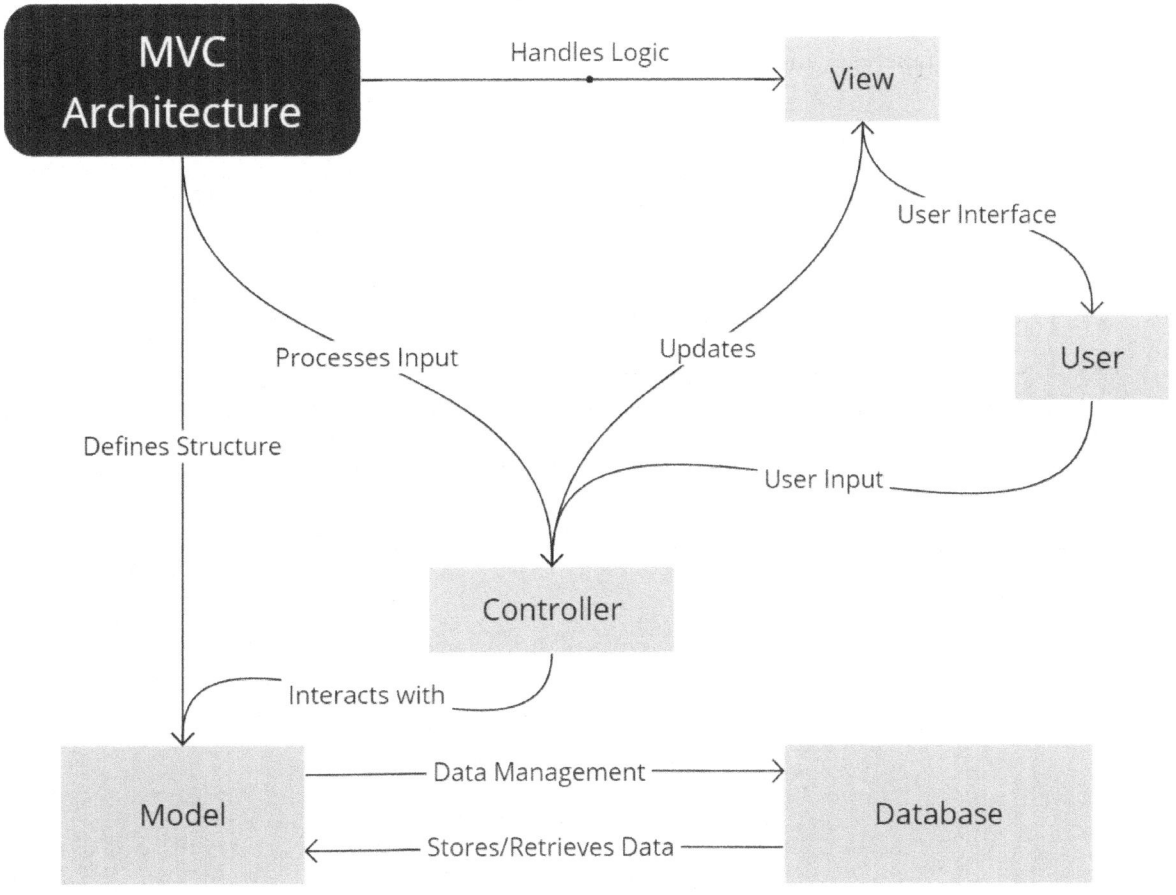

Fig 2.3 MVC Architecture in Go

Applying MVC to GitforGits Bookstore

The heart of our application, the model, would include data structures related to books, users, orders, and reviews. Residing within pkg/models, they would interact with the database, ensuring data consistency, validation, and business logic. For example, the book.go file might contain the book struct, methods to retrieve books, add new books, or modify existing ones.

The view, focusing on user interaction, would be implemented within web/templates. Using Go's template package, these templates would render dynamic content. A booklist.html might display available books, while userdashboard.html presents a user's order history and recommendations.

These templates, combined with static assets in web/static, construct the visual layer of the Bookstore.

Controllers, potentially residing within internal/handlers, handle HTTP requests, bridging the Model and View. For instance, bookHandler.go might process user requests related to books – fetching a list of books, retrieving a specific book's details, or processing a new book review. These controllers take user input, interact with the model, and provide data to the views for rendering.

The power of MVC lies in the interplay between its components. For GitforGits Bookstore, when a user browses a list of books, the flow is as follows:
- User sends a request, which the controller handles.
- The controller interacts with the model, fetching a list of books.
- The model retrieves the data and sends it back to the controller.
- The controller then provides this data to the view.
- The view renders a page displaying the list of books to the user.

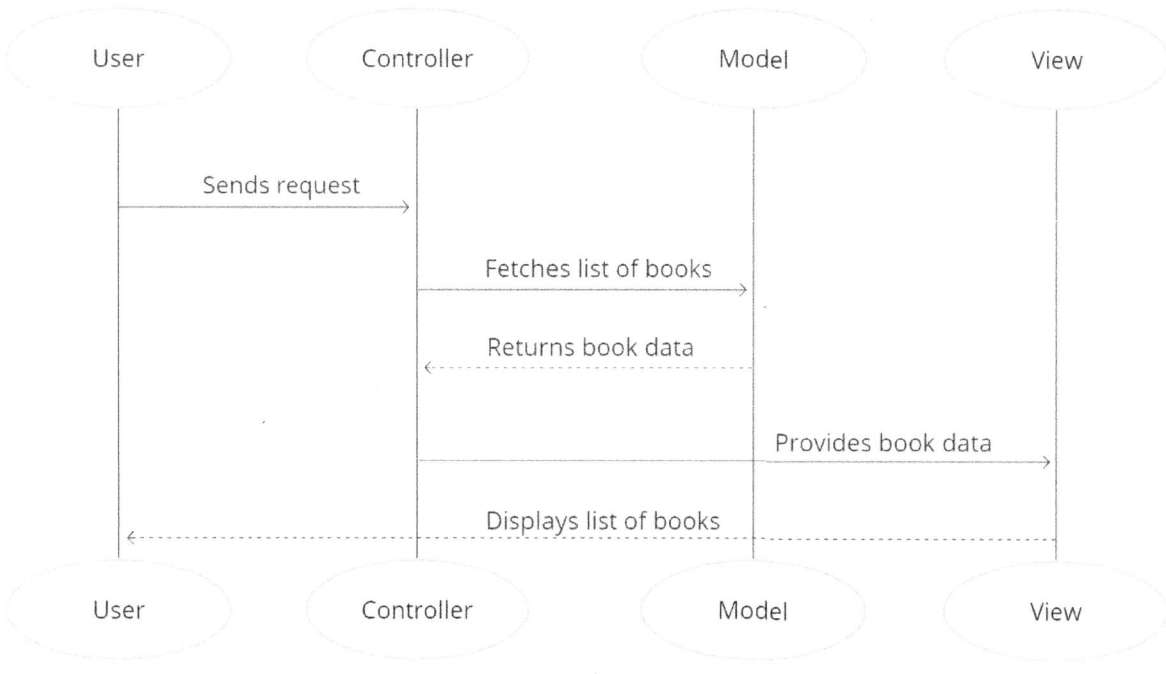

Fig 2.4 Application Flow

By compartmentalizing responsibilities, MVC provides a logical roadmap for development and also ensures the application remains scalable, maintainable, and robust.

Programming Main Application Object

The central hub, also known as the orchestrator, is the primary application object in web development. It is responsible for bringing together various application settings, including routes, handlers, middleware, and other components. This particular object serves as the fulcrum for the GitforGits Bookstore Web App. Its purpose is to guarantee that when a user interacts with our service, everything else operates without any problems. The life cycle of our application is managed by this object, which also handles incoming requests and decides how responses should be crafted and sent back to the user.

Defining Application Object Structure

In order to properly conceptualize the structure of our application object, it is essential to do so before beginning to write code. The following should be contained within this object:

- Routes: Clear paths that map to various functionalities like viewing a book, creating a user account, or placing an order.
- Middleware: Functions or utilities executed before hitting our main handlers—such as logging requests or verifying user authentication.
- Configuration: Settings vital for our application, possibly loaded from a configuration file or environment variables.
- Database Connections: Active connections to our data store, facilitating data fetches, updates, and deletions.

Crafting Main Application Object

```go
package main

import (
    "database/sql"
    "net/http"
    "github.com/gorilla/mux"
)

type App struct {
    Router  *mux.Router
    DB      *sql.DB
    Config  map[string]string
}
```

```go
func (a *App) Initialize(config map[string]string) {
    // Database Connection Logic
    connectionString := config["database"]
    var err error
    a.DB, err = sql.Open("mysql", connectionString)
    if err != nil {
        panic(err)
    }

    // Initialize Router and Routes
    a.Router = mux.NewRouter()
    a.initializeRoutes()
}

func (a *App) initializeRoutes() {
    a.Router.HandleFunc("/books", a.getBooks).Methods("GET")
    // ... more routes to be added
}

func (a *App) getBooks(w http.ResponseWriter, r *http.Request) {
    // Handler logic to fetch and return list of books
}

func (a *App) Run(addr string) {
    http.ListenAndServe(addr, a.Router)
}

func main() {
    config := map[string]string{
        "database": "user:password@/dbname",
    }
```

```
    app := &App{}
    app.Initialize(config)
    app.Run(":8080")
}
```

Decoding the Script
- The Application Structure: Our App struct encapsulates the Router, a connection to the database, and configuration details.
- Initialization: The Initialize method takes care of the foundational setup. It connects to the database and sets up the main router.
- Routes: Using the powerful gorilla/mux package, we initiate routing. The initializeRoutes method maps different routes to their respective handlers.
- Handlers: Functions like getBooks are where the application's main logic resides. This function, for instance, would query our database for books and return them to the user.
- Running the Application: The Run method starts our server, listening on a given address and serving requests via the defined router.
- The Main Function: This is where our application kicks off. We define configurations, create an instance of our App, initialize it, and finally, run it.

There is still more work to be done in order to create a full-fledged application, despite the fact that the setup described above provides an elementary look into the main application object. Additional enhancements to our application would include the addition of middleware functions, error handling mechanisms, and richer configurations (which could be derived from environment variables or configuration files). In order to add logging middleware, for example, it would be necessary to modify the Initialize method and implement new functions in order to process each and every request that is received.

Configuration and Environment Variables

The ability to externalize settings from the application code is made possible for developers by means of configuration files or environment variables. Runtime settings such as port numbers, database connection details, and API keys are examples of what might fall under this category. Through the process of externalizing configurations of this kind, an application can become more flexible and adaptable to a variety of environments, including production, testing, and development environments.

At the operating system level, environment variables are a subset of configuration that control the environment. They are key-value pairs that can be accessed by software that is currently operating on the system. It is possible to make modifications to them without having to modify the application code, which is their greatest strength. When it comes to sensitive information, such as database passwords or API keys, this is especially helpful because it ensures that such essential data is not hard-coded into the application.

Implementing Configuration and Environment Variables

The os package, which is provided by the standard library of Go, is equipped with functionalities that allow them to interact with the underlying operating system. These functionalities include the ability to retrieve environment variables.

During the process of local development, it is convenient to use a .env file to simulate the environment variables that will be set on production systems. These variables will be set at the operating system level. There is a package called godotenv that gives developers the ability to load environment variables into the Go application from a .env file.

```go
package main

import (
    "os"
    "log"
    "github.com/joho/godotenv"
)

type Configuration struct {
    ServerAddress  string
    DbUser         string
    DbPassword     string
    DbHost         string
    DbName         string
}

func loadConfiguration() Configuration {
    // Load .env file during local development
    err := godotenv.Load(".env")
    if err != nil {
        log.Println("Error loading .env file, assuming production environment with OS level environment variables")
    }
```

```go
    return Configuration{
        ServerAddress: os.Getenv("SERVER_ADDRESS"),
        DbUser:     os.Getenv("DB_USER"),
        DbPassword: os.Getenv("DB_PASSWORD"),
        DbHost:     os.Getenv("DB_HOST"),
        DbName:     os.Getenv("DB_NAME"),
    }
}

func main() {
    config := loadConfiguration()
    // Use the configuration throughout the application
    // ...
}
```

In the code snippet above:
- The Configuration struct represents our application's configuration, sourced from environment variables.
- The loadConfiguration function uses godotenv to load variables from the .env file (during local development) and then uses the os package to fetch these variables.
- Finally, in the main function, we load our configuration, ready to be used throughout our application.

While implementing it at my end, I came across couple of errors and so would always advise following tips:
- Never Commit .env: While the .env file is invaluable in local development, it should never be committed to version control systems like git. It might contain sensitive information.
- Hierarchical Configuration: Sometimes, configurations might have a hierarchy – default values, overridden by environment variables, and perhaps further overridden by command-line flags. Plan the hierarchy judiciously.
- Clear Naming Conventions: Ensure that environment variable names are clear and self-explanatory. For instance, GITFORGITS_DB_USER is clearer than GFG_DB_U.

Configuration and environment variables ensure that our GitforGits Bookstore Web App remains adaptable to varied environments and keeps sensitive data shielded. As we delve deeper into building our web app, this foundation will continually prove instrumental in ensuring a seamless, efficient, and secure development and deployment process.

Dependency Injection
Overview
One of the most important design patterns in software engineering is known as Dependency Injection (DI), which plays a crucial role in achieving Inversion of Control (IoC) between classes and the dependencies that they have. It is an essential component in the evolution of a decoupled architecture, which is characterized by the independence and modularity of its components. DI refers to the process of providing components with their dependencies externally, as opposed to having them construct dependencies through their own internal processes. Generally speaking, this is accomplished through the use of constructors, methods, or property setters.

One of the most important aspects of DI is its capacity to invert control structure. The creation and management of a component's dependencies have traditionally been the responsibility of the component. DI, on the other hand, transfers this responsibility. A component's dependencies are "injected" into it from the outside, typically during the runtime of the component. Taking this approach not only makes the design of the component easier to understand, but it also improves modularity and encourages the separation of concerns.

Benefits of Dependency Injection
- Decoupling of Components: DI is able to significantly reduce the tight coupling that exists between the various components of an application, which results in decoupling of those components. Instead of relying on concrete implementations of their dependencies, components are specifically designed to depend on abstractions, also known as interfaces. Using this abstraction, components become more interchangeable and adaptable to changes in the environment.
- Enhancement of Testability: The ease with which DI can be tested is one of the most notable advantages of this development methodology. By injecting dependencies, it is possible to easily replace actual implementations with mock objects or stubs. This is made available by injecting dependencies. Having this isolation makes it possible to conduct unit tests that are more focused, allowing the focus to be on the logic of the component rather than its dependencies.
- Flexibility and Maintainability: With DI, the configuration of components is externalized from the components themselves, which allows for greater flexibility and maintainability. Because of this separation, any modifications that are made to the configuration or the implementation of a dependency do not require any changes to be made to the component that is the recipient of those modifications. Applications end up becoming more adaptable and less difficult to maintain as a consequence of this.
- Lifecycle Management: Containers that manage the lifecycle of dependencies are frequently used to facilitate a distributed infrastructure (DI). In order to maximize the

utilization of resources and the management of those resources, these containers determine when to create new instances or reuse existing ones. The automated management of lifecycles is especially useful in complex applications, where the manual management of object lifecycles can be prone to errors and can be a burdensome process.
- Scalability and Integration: As applications expand, DI makes it simpler to incorporate new components or services into the software development process. Increasing the size of the application or integrating services provided by third parties becomes easier to manage when components are not tightly coupled to one another.
- Consistency and Standardization: DI encourages a consistent and standardized approach to managing dependencies across an application, which makes it possible to achieve greater consistency and standardization. The application of this uniformity is advantageous, particularly in large teams, because it establishes a distinct pattern for developers to adhere to.

Implementing Dependency Injection

Utilizing DI in Go doesn't necessarily require complex frameworks. Go's interfaces and the language's composability make DI simpler and straightforward.

Consider a simple example relating to our bookstore:

```go
type BookRepository interface {
    GetByID(id int) (*Book, error)
}

type SQLBookRepository struct {
    db *sql.DB
}

func (s *SQLBookRepository) GetByID(id int) (*Book, error) {
    // Implementation using SQL database
}

type BookService struct {
    repo BookRepository
}

func NewBookService(r BookRepository) *BookService {
```

```go
    return &BookService{repo: r}
}

func main() {
    db := //... initialization of the database
    sqlRepo := &SQLBookRepository{db: db}
    bookService := NewBookService(sqlRepo)
    // Use the bookService
}
```

In the above code snippet:
- BookRepository is an interface that any book-related data source must implement.
- SQLBookRepository is a concrete implementation using an SQL database.
- BookService contains business logic related to books, with its data source (or repository) injected.
- The main function showcases DI in action. We initialize the SQL repository and inject it into the BookService.

Health Check Endpoints

URLs that have been specifically designed for use within a web application and that return the status of the system are known as health check endpoints. These endpoints, when accessed, provide a quick snapshot of the system's health, indicating whether or not all of the components and dependencies are functioning as expected.

Setting up Health Check Endpoints
Basic Health Check

A rudimentary health check merely indicates if the service is running. It doesn't verify if all dependencies (like databases or external services) are operational but provides a quick way to ascertain if the application instance is responsive.

```go
func (a *App) healthCheckHandler(w http.ResponseWriter, r *http.Request) {
    w.WriteHeader(http.StatusOK)
    w.Write([]byte("OK"))
}

// During route initialization:
```

```go
a.Router.HandleFunc("/healthcheck", a.healthCheckHandler).Methods("GET")
```

When accessing /healthcheck, the service will respond with a 200 OK status and the message "OK".

Advanced Health Check

Besides verifying the service's status, a more thorough health check also verifies its dependencies. This could mean checking the health of the database, ensuring connectivity to external services, or even determining the status of internal caches for GitforGits Bookstore.

```go
func (a *App) detailedHealthCheckHandler(w http.ResponseWriter, r *http.Request) {
    // Check database health
    if err := a.DB.Ping(); err != nil {
        w.WriteHeader(http.StatusInternalServerError)
        w.Write([]byte("Database Unreachable"))
        return
    }

    // Additional checks (external services, cache systems, etc.) can be added here

    w.WriteHeader(http.StatusOK)
    w.Write([]byte("OK"))
}

// During route initialization:
a.Router.HandleFunc("/detailed-healthcheck",
a.detailedHealthCheckHandler).Methods("GET")
```

Accessing or performing a detailed-health check provides a set of validations. If any check fails, it returns an error message indicating the problematic component. While health checks are valuable, exposing detailed system information can be a security concern. It's wise to secure detailed health check endpoints, ensuring only authorized personnel or systems can access them.

These above endpoints offer a proactive mechanism to detect issues, potentially even before they impact users, ensuring that the digital bookstore provides a seamless, uninterrupted experience to its audience.

Summary

This chapter provided a comprehensive examination of the fundamental principles that govern the development and maintenance of web applications that are considered to be resilient. We began by gaining an understanding of the critical significance of configurations and environment variables, thereby highlighting the requirement of separating settings from the primary application. Both the application's adaptability and its level of security are improved by these configurations, regardless of whether they pertain to the details of the database connection or to the API keys. It is possible for the GitforGits Bookstore Web App to achieve seamless adaptability to a variety of environments because it does not make use of configurations that are hard-coded. Consequently, this makes it possible to have more seamless transitions between the phases of development, testing, and production.

We started off by learning about configurations, and then we moved on to the more complicated aspects of Dependency Injection (DI), which is a paradigm that places an emphasis on the separation of application components and the dependencies between them. The GitforGits Bookstore has the potential to reap significant benefits from Dependency Injection (DI), including the attainment of modularity, enhanced testability, and improved maintainability. Through the examination of specific examples, we were able to observe how Dependency Injection (DI) contributes to the development of a codebase that is well-organized, modular, and optimized. This allows components to keep their independence while simultaneously facilitating interactions that are seamless within the larger application ecosystem.

In the following section, the chapter proceeded to investigate the significant field of health check endpoints, highlighting the significance of these endpoints in terms of monitoring and maintaining the health of web services. As the guardians of the application, these endpoints perform a variety of checks, ranging from straightforward checks that validate the responsiveness of the service to comprehensive checks that validate multiple dependencies. They provide information that is both immediate and up to date regarding the state of the system, which enables prompt actions to be taken in the event that abnormalities occur. With regard to the GitforGits Bookstore, these health checks are absolutely necessary. As the platform grows and supports a greater number of users, they make certain that any potential issues are quickly identified and resolved at the earliest possible opportunity. Keeping a seamless and optimal user experience is made easier as a result of this.

Chapter 3: Handling HTTP Requests and Routing

Backbone of Web

HTTP, or HyperText Transfer Protocol, is the bedrock of data communication on the World Wide Web. In essence, it establishes the rules for transferring files (text, images, video, etc.) on the web. Its design allows clients—typically web browsers—to communicate with servers to request and receive data.

HTTP Requests and Routing

When a user enters a URL into a browser or clicks a link, an HTTP request is made. This request is directed towards a web server that interprets the request and responds accordingly. At the heart of this interpretation is routing. Routing determines how an application responds to a client request for a specific endpoint, which is a URI (or path) and a specific HTTP request method (like GET, POST, etc.).

For web applications like the GitforGits Bookstore, routing is foundational. The web application must discern between a request to view a list of books, see details of a specific book, edit a book, or delete one. Each of these actions corresponds to a unique combination of a URI and an HTTP method. The router in our application would analyze incoming requests and route them to the appropriate handler functions based on this combination.

HTTP Methods

HTTP methods, often termed as "verbs," define the kind of action a request intends to perform. These methods provide a semantic way to describe the primary action behind an HTTP request.

Following is a brief overview:
- GET: It's the most common method, used to request data from a server. For instance, when a user wants to view a book's details on GitforGits Bookstore, a GET request is made. It only retrieves data and doesn't modify it.
- POST: This method submits data to be processed to a specified resource. In the context of our bookstore, when a user creates a new account or adds a review for a book, a POST request is issued. Unlike GET, it modifies data on the server.
- PUT: Used to update an existing resource or create it if it doesn't exist. If a user wanted to update their account details or change a book review, a PUT request would be ideal. It ensures idempotence; making the same request multiple times results in the same outcome.
- DELETE: As the name suggests, this method deletes the specified resource. If a user wanted to delete a book review or remove a book from their wishlist, the application would utilize a DELETE request.
- HEAD: Similar to GET, but it only retrieves the headers of the response, not the actual data. It's useful when one only needs meta-information about a resource.

- PATCH: Used to apply partial modifications to a resource. If a user wanted to update just their email address but leave other account details unchanged, a PATCH request could be employed.
- OPTIONS: This method describes the communication options for the target resource. It provides information about the communication possibilities and is a way to ascertain the capabilities of a web server.

In the GitforGits Bookstore application, each of these HTTP methods plays a distinct role, ensuring users can interact with the platform seamlessly. From merely browsing books (GET) to adding them to a cart (POST) or updating user details (PATCH/PUT), these methods ensure every action is captured, processed, and responded to with precision.

Navigate User Interactions

Request-Response Paradigm

The internet's foundation lies in a dance of requests and responses. When a user performs an action online, like clicking on a link to view a book's details, they're essentially sending a request to a server. This server processes the request and sends back a response, which might be the book's details or an error message if the book isn't available. This iterative process of requesting and receiving is ubiquitous, powering every interaction on the web.

Request Phase

Imagine a user, Alice, browsing the GitforGits Bookstore. She's intrigued by a new novel and clicks on its title to see more.

At this click:
- Initiation: Alice's browser initiates an HTTP GET request. This request is directed to the server hosting the GitforGits Bookstore, specifically asking for details about the novel.
- Header Composition: Along with the primary request, the browser sends headers containing meta-information, like browser type or any cookies associated with GitforGits.
- Routing: As the request reaches the server, the application's router takes over. It discerns that Alice is asking for book details based on the URL and the GET method.
- Handler Invocation: Post routing, the request lands in a handler – a function designed to fetch book details.

Response Phase

Once the server receives Alice's request:
1. Handler Logic: The handler function communicates with the database, fetching the novel's details.
2. Crafting the Response: With the details fetched, the server crafts an HTTP response. This

includes:
- o Status Code: A code indicating the result of the request, e.g., 200 for success or 404 if the book isn't found.
- o Headers: Meta-information, like the type of content being sent back (e.g., HTML or JSON).
- o Body: The actual content, in this case, the novel's details.
3. Sending the Response: This crafted response travels back to Alice's browser.
4. Browser Rendering: Upon receipt, Alice's browser interprets the response. It reads the headers to understand the content type and subsequently renders the novel's details on the screen for Alice.

Beyond fetching book details, the request-response cycle powers multiple interactions in the GitforGits Bookstore:

- User Account Creation: A user might fill in a registration form and click 'Register'. This action sends a POST request with the user's data. The server processes this, creates an account, and responds, either confirming account creation or detailing any issues.
- Adding to Cart: When a user adds a book to their cart, a POST or PUT request is made. The server updates the cart and responds, perhaps by refreshing the cart's view to show the newly added book.
- Reviews and Ratings: Submitting a review for a book would typically be a POST request, with the user's rating and comments sent to the server. The server would update the book's reviews and respond, possibly by displaying the new review.

The request-response cycle can be thought of as a conversation that takes place between a user and a server. This conversation is triggered off with each and every click and action that is performed on the GitforGits Bookstore. The interaction is harmonious, with users expressing their requests and the server responding to those requests.

Handlers and HandlerFuncs

When it comes to managing incoming HTTP requests, handlers are an essential component of the net/http package that needs to be utilized. Any object that satisfies the requirements of the http.Handler interface is considered to be a handler. One method, namely ServeHTTP(ResponseWriter, *Request), is required to be used for this interface. It stipulates that any type that implements this method is capable of performing the function of a handler, which functions to process HTTP requests and send back responses.

Understanding HandlerFuncs

While defining a whole new type to satisfy the http.Handler interface might seem cumbersome for simple applications or individual routes, Go offers a shortcut: the http.HandlerFunc type. This is essentially a type alias for a function with the signature func(ResponseWriter, *Request). It lets developers write standalone functions as handlers without creating new types. What's even more powerful is that http.HandlerFunc has a ServeHTTP method, enabling it to satisfy the http.Handler interface, providing immense flexibility.

We shall consider a scenario where a user wants to view a list of books. This action would necessitate a handler that retrieves the list from a database and displays it.

```
func BookListHandler(w http.ResponseWriter, r *http.Request) {
    books := getBooksFromDatabase() // Fetch the books
    renderBooks(w, books)           // Render the books to the user
}
```

To use this handler with the default Go HTTP router, you'd register it as: http.HandleFunc("/books", BookListHandler).

If a user clicks on a specific book to view its details, a handler catering to this request becomes essential.

```
func BookDetailHandler(w http.ResponseWriter, r *http.Request) {
    bookID := r.URL.Query().Get("id")  // Get the book ID from the URL query parameters
    book := getBookByID(bookID)        // Fetch the specific book
    renderBookDetail(w, book)          // Render the book's details to the user
}
```

The process of registering this would be comparable to the following: http.HandleFunc("/book", BookDetailHandler).

Consider a scenario where we want to log every request to the GitforGits Bookstore:

```
func LoggingMiddleware(next http.Handler) http.Handler {
    return http.HandlerFunc(func(w http.ResponseWriter, r *http.Request) {
        log.Printf("Request received: %s %s", r.Method, r.URL.Path)
        next.ServeHTTP(w, r)  // Pass on to the next handler
    })
}
```

To use this middleware, you'd wrap your handler: loggedHandler := LoggingMiddleware(BookListHandler).

Go's design encourages function composition, and this extends to handlers as well. You can wrap handlers within other handlers, building a stack of functionalities that a request passes through. For instance, besides logging, you might want authentication.

Explore Routes

Just for a moment, picture a monumental city with a complex system of roads, alleys, and highways. These pathways direct vehicles and pedestrians to their destinations, and similarly, routes in web applications direct user requests to their intended destinations. Routes are the relationship that is defined between the URLs (or URIs) that users request and the code that is responsible for handling these requests. Routes are at the core of a web application.

Routes as Connectors

Take, for example, a user who is looking for a particular book and finds themselves on the GitforGits Bookstore website. They might begin their journey through the digital world by entering a URL or clicking on a link provided to them. The URL is connected to a particular handler on the server through the assistance of routes, which serve as the directing force in this journey. Because of this connection, the server is able to determine precisely which section of code should be responsible for processing the request. The absence of routing would result in web applications that are devoid of structure and clarity, which would result in an experience that is both cumbersome and unfriendly to users.

Route Patterns and Dynamic Routing

In contrast to the straightforward nature of static routes such as /books or /contact, the dynamic nature of modern web applications frequently necessitates the implementation of more complex routing patterns. As an illustration, the URL could be formatted as /book/:id in order to view a particular book contained within GitforGits. This is a dynamic route that is able to handle multiple URLs such as /book/1, /book/2, and so on because the variable ':id' serves as a placeholder in this instance. Every one of the IDs is associated with a different book, which makes it possible for a single route to dynamically retrieve information about a variety of books. This approach not only makes the codebase easier to understand and manage, but it also improves its scalability and maintainability.

At GitforGits, for example, if the only users who are permitted to add book reviews are those who are logged in, then middleware that is attached to the /add-review route can verify user authentication. Only in the event that the user has been authenticated does it process the request; otherwise, it will redirect the user to a login page. The routing system receives an additional layer of functionality and security as a result of this.

Route Grouping and Hierarchical Routing

It is possible for the number of routes to significantly increase as web applications continue to expand. In order to effectively manage this complexity, routes frequently support hierarchical or grouping structures. According to GitforGits, for instance, all book-related routes could be grouped together under a parent route called "books," with sub-routes such as "books/fiction" and "books/history." Not only does this hierarchical approach to routing make the codebase easier to understand, but it also makes route management procedures more efficient. It offers a user experience that is more organized and intuitive, which makes it simpler for users to navigate the application.

By quietly and effectively directing the flow of user requests, routes in a web application are comparable to the unseen workforce that is working behind the scenes. They take measures to ensure that every interaction, whether it be browsing, purchasing, reviewing, or exploring, is handled with precision and accuracy.

Routes Programming

Setting up Routes

As users navigate GitforGits Bookstore, each URL they access should correspond to a specific function or piece of code that dictates the application's behavior for that URL.

```
http.HandleFunc("/books", BookListHandler)
```

In the snippet above, when a user accesses the /books URL, the BookListHandler function is invoked, which could display a list of books available in the bookstore.

Dynamic Routes and Route Variables

For a bookstore, static routes won't suffice. If a user wants to view details of a specific book, the URL would likely contain the book's ID or title. Such dynamic routes can be crafted with third-party routers like gorilla/mux, a popular choice for Go developers.

```
r := mux.NewRouter()
r.HandleFunc("/book/{id:[0-9]+}", BookDetailHandler)
```

With gorilla/mux, the route pattern /book/{id:[0-9]+} captures numerical IDs and passes them to BookDetailHandler. Inside this handler, you can retrieve the id to fetch and display the corresponding book's details. Over the period as the GitforGits Bookstore grows, categorizing routes becomes crucial. For instance, all book-related routes could be grouped under a /books prefix.

```
bookRouter := r.PathPrefix("/books").Subrouter()
bookRouter.HandleFunc("/", AllBooksHandler)
bookRouter.HandleFunc("/{id:[0-9]+}", BookDetailHandler)
bookRouter.HandleFunc("/{id:[0-9]+}/reviews", BookReviewHandler)
```

This structure neatly compartmentalizes book-related functionalities, ensuring the code remains organized and scalable.

Middleware in Routing

Middleware functions operate before the primary handler, allowing for pre-processing of requests. A common use-case of middleware for GitforGits might be user authentication.

```
func AuthenticationMiddleware(next http.Handler) http.Handler {
    return http.HandlerFunc(func(w http.ResponseWriter, r *http.Request) {
        if !userIsAuthenticated(r) {
            http.Redirect(w, r, "/login", 302)
            return
        }
        next.ServeHTTP(w, r)
    })
}

bookRouter.Use(AuthenticationMiddleware)
```

With the above, every request passing through bookRouter undergoes authentication. If a user isn't logged in, they're redirected to the login page.

Error Handling and Custom 404 Pages

By default, web servers provide generic error messages, but these are often not user-friendly or informative enough to guide users effectively. Custom error handling, especially in the context of using frameworks like gorilla/mux in Go, allows developers to provide more meaningful, user-centric error responses. This approach not only enhances the user experience but also offers a more professional and polished look to your application.

When a user encounters an error, the default server response can be confusing or unhelpful. Custom error handling transforms this experience. It involves detecting errors and responding with messages or pages that are specifically designed to be helpful and relevant to the user's context. For instance, in the GitforGits Bookstore, if a user tries to access a non-existent book page, instead of a stark "404 Not Found" message, they could be greeted with a custom page suggesting similar books or a search bar to find what they're looking for. For example, Gorilla/mux simplifies the process of setting up custom error handlers. It allows developers to define what should happen when an HTTP error occurs. For example, a custom 404 page can be set up to handle requests to unknown routes as below:

```go
func NotFoundHandler(w http.ResponseWriter, r *http.Request) {
    w.WriteHeader(http.StatusNotFound)
    w.Write([]byte("Book not found. Visit our catalog to explore other books."))
}

r.NotFoundHandler = http.HandlerFunc(NotFoundHandler)
```

Whenever a user accesses an invalid URL or a non-existent book, the NotFoundHandler provides a friendly message guiding them back.

With libraries like gorilla/mux, Go's flexibility allows developers to create routes that are intuitive, dynamic, and efficient. The users' experience is guaranteed to be smooth, well-organized, and enjoyable as they make their way through the bookstore thanks to these suggested routes. Every URL that they visit, every book that they investigate, and every review that they read is made possible by routes that have been meticulously programmed. These routes serve as the silent sentinels that guide and enhance every interaction.

URL Parameters

The creation of dynamic and interactive web applications is made possible by URL parameters, which are an essential component of web development and play a crucial role in the process. Additionally, they make it possible for data to be transmitted through URLs, which enables the customization of user experiences based on the actions or inputs of the user. When it comes to the development of web applications, there are primarily two categories of URL parameters: Query Parameters and Path Parameters (also known as Route Variables). Each of these categories serves a distinct function.

Types of URL Parameters

1. Query Parameters: Often seen after a ? in URLs, these parameters follow the format key=value. For instance, in gitforgits.com/books?genre=fiction, genre is the key, and fiction its value. Multiple query parameters can be chained using &.
2. Path Parameters (or Route Variables): These are embedded within the URL path itself.

For example, in gitforgits.com/book/1234, 1234 is a path parameter representing a specific book's ID.

For GitforGits Bookstore:
- Query Parameters might filter book listings: gitforgits.com/books?author=doe could display books only by author 'Doe'.
- Path Parameters would identify unique entities: gitforgits.com/book/5678 would detail the book with ID 5678.

Implementing Dynamic URL Parameters

Harnessing a router like gorilla/mux can streamline the implementation of dynamic URL parameters.

Setting up Path Parameters

Path parameters allow URLs to be flexible and dynamic. Consider a URL to view a specific book in the GitforGits bookstore:

```
r := mux.NewRouter()
r.HandleFunc("/book/{id:[0-9]+}", BookDetailHandler)
```

In the above, {id:[0-9]+} is a path parameter, capturing any numerical ID. Inside BookDetailHandler, you can retrieve this value:

```
func BookDetailHandler(w http.ResponseWriter, r *http.Request) {
    vars := mux.Vars(r)
    bookID := vars["id"]
    // Use bookID to fetch and display the book's details
}
```

Utilizing Query Parameters

Query parameters are key for filtering or sorting lists. If a user wants to view books of a specific genre, called fantasy:
URL: gitforgits.com/books?genre=fantasy

To capture and use this in Go:

```
func BookListHandler(w http.ResponseWriter, r *http.Request) {
```

```
    genre := r.URL.Query().Get("genre")
    // Use the genre value to filter and display a list of books
}
```

For multiple query parameters, iterate over r.URL.Query() to handle each. Often, web applications combine both parameter types. In the context of GitforGits, users might want to view reviews of a specific book written after a certain date, such as:
URL: gitforgits.com/book/5678/reviews?after=2023-01-01

Both the book ID (path parameter) and the date (query parameter) influence the content displayed. By understanding and implementing dynamic URL parameters, developers empower the bookstore to be more than a static platform. It becomes a fluid, responsive entity, always ready to cater to each user's unique literary journey.

Grouping Routes
Overview
The concept of grouping routes in web applications revolves around the organization. Without categorized shelves for fiction, non-fiction, fantasy, or history, locating a book would be chaotic. Similarly, in web applications, as the number of endpoints increases, clustering related endpoints ensures clarity, scalability, and maintainability.

Grouping routes serves multiple purposes:
- Code Organization: By bundling related endpoints, developers can maintain a structured and logical codebase. This enhances readability and eases maintenance.
- Middleware Application: Certain middleware might be relevant only for specific groups. By clustering related routes, applying middleware selectively becomes straightforward.
- Scalability: As applications expand, adding new routes or modifying existing ones is more manageable when they're organized logically.
- Consistent URL Patterns: Grouped routes lead to intuitive URL patterns. For users and developers alike, predicting or remembering URLs becomes simpler.

Sample Program: Structuring Endpoints
Harnessing a powerful router like gorilla/mux can make route grouping intuitive.

Book-Related Routes
Given that books form the crux of the GitforGits Bookstore, let us try to have a dedicated route group.

```go
bookRouter := r.PathPrefix("/books").Subrouter()

// List all books
bookRouter.HandleFunc("/", AllBooksHandler)

// Detail a specific book by ID
bookRouter.HandleFunc("/{id:[0-9]+}", BookDetailHandler)

// Fetch reviews for a specific book
bookRouter.HandleFunc("/{id:[0-9]+}/reviews", BookReviewsHandler)
```

These endpoints, logically clustered under /books, deal exclusively with books, offering listing, detailed view, and review access.

User Account Management

A bookstore application requires user account management for actions like registration, login, and profile access.

```go
userRouter := r.PathPrefix("/users").Subrouter()

// User registration
userRouter.HandleFunc("/register", RegisterHandler)

// User login
userRouter.HandleFunc("/login", LoginHandler)

// View user profile
userRouter.HandleFunc("/profile", ProfileHandler)
```

Grouped under /users, these routes handle user-related functionalities, ensuring a seamless user experience.

Order and Cart Management

Users will likely wish to manage their cart, check out books, or view past orders.

```go
orderRouter := r.PathPrefix("/orders").Subrouter()

// View cart
orderRouter.HandleFunc("/cart", CartHandler)

// Checkout process
orderRouter.HandleFunc("/checkout", CheckoutHandler)

// View past orders
orderRouter.HandleFunc("/history", OrderHistoryHandler)
```

Bundling these under /orders captures all actions related to buying books, streamlining the user's shopping journey.

Middleware and Grouped Routes

One of the pivotal advantages of grouped routes is the streamlined application of middleware. For instance, every endpoint under the userRouter might necessitate user authentication. By applying an authentication middleware solely to userRouter, you ensure each related endpoint inherits this authentication check without individually attaching the middleware.

```go
userRouter.Use(AuthenticationMiddleware)
```

Grouped routes instill order, logic, and structure in web applications. In the ongoing GitforGits Bookstore application, as readers explore titles, authors, genres, or their user profiles, grouped routes ensure their journey remains intuitive. Every URL they access, from book listings to user settings, is structured, offering a coherent user experience.

Navigate Web Routing with Gorilla/Mux

In the extensive ecosystem of Go's libraries, gorilla/mux stands out as the foremost routing library. Renowned for its flexibility, performance, and ease of use, it's the de facto choice for many Go developers when building web applications. While Go's standard library offers basic routing functionalities, gorilla/mux elevates this with features like path parameters, advanced matching, and middleware support, making it a staple for sophisticated web projects like GitforGits Bookstore.

Setting up Gorilla/Mux

Installation

To integrate gorilla/mux into your project, you need to install it first:

go get -u github.com/gorilla/mux

Executing the above command fetches the gorilla/mux library and adds it to your Go project.

Initialization and Basic Routing

Once installed, initializing a new router with gorilla/mux is a breeze.

```go
package main

import (
    "net/http"
    "github.com/gorilla/mux"
)

func main() {
    r := mux.NewRouter()

    // Basic route
    r.HandleFunc("/", HomeHandler)

    // Start the server
    http.ListenAndServe(":8080", r)
}
```

In this snippet, a new mux router is created and a basic route (/) is associated with the HomeHandler function.

Advanced Route Matching

The power of gorilla/mux becomes evident when defining complex routes.

```go
// Route with a path parameter
r.HandleFunc("/book/{id:[0-9]+}", BookDetailHandler)
```

```go
// Route restricted to a specific HTTP method
r.HandleFunc("/book/add", AddBookHandler).Methods("POST")
```

In these examples, the first route captures numerical book IDs, while the second route is specifically for POST requests to add a new book.

Middleware Integration

Building on previous learnings, integrating middleware with gorilla/mux is intuitive. For GitforGits, an authentication middleware for user-related routes can be implemented as:

```go
userRouter := r.PathPrefix("/users").Subrouter()
userRouter.Use(AuthenticationMiddleware)
```

Every route under userRouter will now be processed by AuthenticationMiddleware before reaching its designated handler.

Configuring Gorilla/Mux for Optimal Performance

For large-scale applications including GitforGits Bookstore, fine-tuning configurations ensures peak performance. The SkipClean option, when set, prevents the router from cleaning URLs. While this can offer performance boosts, caution is advised as unclean URLs can lead to unforeseen behaviors.

```go
r := mux.NewRouter().SkipClean(true)
```

Despite the fact that the bookstore is growing, this powerful library guarantees that the routing process will continue to be streamlined, organized, and effective. Because every book that is added, every user that registers, and every review that is written will be routed in a seamless manner, users will have access to an unparalleled browsing experience.

Error Handling in Go

Mistakes can happen in any web app, no matter how well-designed or complicated it is. How these apps deal with these kinds of surprises greatly influences how users view and interact with them. The 404 (Not Found) and 500 (Internal Server Error) statuses are two of the most common types of errors encountered in web applications. The 404 error typically occurs when a user attempts to access a page or resource that does not exist, possibly as a result of a mistyped URL or a broken link, whereas the 500 error is a more general server-side error indicating that something has gone wrong on the website's server. Both of these errors, if not handled correctly, can result in user frustration and a loss of user trust.

Web developers can significantly improve the user experience by addressing these errors in a user-friendly manner, such as through custom error pages that maintain the site's look and feel, provide clear and helpful information, and offer links to guide users back to active parts of the site. These custom error pages not only mitigate the negative impact of an error, but also provide an opportunity to reinforce the website's branding and potentially even delight users in what would otherwise be a frustrating moment. This approach to error handling is critical in maintaining user engagement and trust, ensuring that even when things go wrong, the user's experience remains positive and seamless.

404 Not Found Error

A 404 error occurs when a user requests a resource (like a web page or an API endpoint) that the server can't locate. For GitforGits Bookstore, this might happen if someone tries accessing a book that doesn't exist.

Out of the box, gorilla/mux offers default error responses. However, to provide a tailored experience, you can set a custom 404 handler.

```go
func CustomNotFoundHandler(w http.ResponseWriter, r *http.Request) {
    w.WriteHeader(http.StatusNotFound)
    w.Write([]byte("Oh no, the book you're seeking seems to be in another shelf! Please try searching again or explore our vast collection."))
}

r := mux.NewRouter()
r.NotFoundHandler = http.HandlerFunc(CustomNotFoundHandler)
```

In this configuration, any non-existent route accessed will invoke CustomNotFoundHandler, giving users a friendly message rather than a stark error.

500 Internal Server Error

A 500 error suggests something went amiss on the server. While reasons vary, from server misconfigurations to application bugs, addressing this error with clarity is crucial. For GitforGits, it ensures users aren't left in the dark when the application encounters internal hiccups.

Handling 500 errors gracefully involves catching panics (unhandled errors that cause the Go application to crash) and responding with a user-friendly message.

```go
func InternalServerErrorHandler(w http.ResponseWriter, r *http.Request) {
    if r := recover(); r != nil {
        w.WriteHeader(http.StatusInternalServerError)
        w.Write([]byte("Oops! Our store seems to have encountered an issue. We're on it. Please revisit in a bit."))
    }
}

r := mux.NewRouter()
r.Use(func(h http.Handler) http.Handler {
    return http.HandlerFunc(func(w http.ResponseWriter, r *http.Request) {
        defer InternalServerErrorHandler(w, r)
        h.ServeHTTP(w, r)
    })
})
```

Using a middleware, the InternalServerErrorHandler captures any panics during request processing and serves a tailored error response.

The distinction between a good and great web application often lies in error handling. For GitforGits Bookstore, addressing 404 and 500 errors with grace and clarity ensures users always feel valued, even amidst technical glitches. Custom error messages infused with the bookstore's personality ensure users stay engaged, fostering loyalty.

Rate Limiting and Request Throttling

Overview

Web applications, like the GitforGits Bookstore, must be able to handle the huge number of requests that come in every millisecond. This is where rate limiting comes in: it's a mechanism that limits the number of requests a user or IP can make to a server within a given time frame. Rate limiting ensures fair usage, protects against DDoS attacks, and maintains a high quality of service for all users by imposing these "speed limits."

Request throttling is a more nuanced technique that is frequently used interchangeably with rate limiting. While rate limiting limits the number of requests, throttling regulates the rate at which they are made. Consider the GitforGits Bookstore's server to be a librarian; if she is bombarded with multiple book queries at once, she will become overwhelmed. Throttling ensures that she answers each query methodically, ensuring that no question goes unanswered.

For GitforGits Bookstore, these mechanisms are pivotal for several reasons:
- Resource Management: Ensures server resources aren't overwhelmed by sudden traffic surges.
- Security: Curtails potential threats by restricting malicious or excessively frequent requests.
- Fair Usage: Ensures all users have equitable access to the bookstore's resources.

Rate Limiting for GitforGits Bookstore

One popular Go middleware for rate limiting is golang.org/x/time/rate. This package provides token bucket-based rate limiting.

Installing the necessary package:

```
go get golang.org/x/time/rate
```

Consider setting a limit of 5 requests per minute for each user.

```go
package main

import (
        "golang.org/x/time/rate"
        "net/http"
        "time"
)

var limiter = rate.NewLimiter(5, 1)

func RateLimit(next http.Handler) http.Handler {
        return http.HandlerFunc(func(w http.ResponseWriter, r *http.Request) {
                if !limiter.Allow() {
                        http.Error(w, "Too many requests", http.StatusTooManyRequests)
                        return
                }
                next.ServeHTTP(w, r)
        })
}
```

This middleware can be applied globally or to specific routes, ensuring those routes adhere to the specified rate limits.

For throttling, middleware can be created to introduce deliberate delays, ensuring a steady request processing pace.

```go
func RequestThrottle(next http.Handler) http.Handler {
    return http.HandlerFunc(func(w http.ResponseWriter, r *http.Request) {
        time.Sleep(200 * time.Millisecond) // Introduce a 200ms delay for every request
        next.ServeHTTP(w, r)
    })
}
```

This approach guarantees the server never gets overwhelmed, even during traffic spikes. Integrating these mechanisms with gorilla/mux and the GitforGits Bookstore is straightforward as shown below:

```go
r := mux.NewRouter()
r.Use(RateLimit, RequestThrottle)

r.HandleFunc("/books", BookListHandler)
r.HandleFunc("/book/{id:[0-9]+}", BookDetailHandler)
```

Once these middlewares are added, all bookstore routes will have global rate limiting and request throttling. Request throttling and rate limiting guard the vast web as millions of readers pour into GitforGits Bookstore. They make sure the online bookstore's system is stable, quick to respond, and powerful.

Performing CRUD Operations
Creating Book
To usher a new book into the GitforGits Bookstore, you'd need an endpoint that supports the creation of book records. Using the POST method ensures data submission for a fresh book.

```go
func CreateBookHandler(w http.ResponseWriter, r *http.Request) {
```

```go
    var newBook Book
    decoder := json.NewDecoder(r.Body)
    err := decoder.Decode(&newBook)
    if err != nil {
        http.Error(w, "Invalid book data", http.StatusBadRequest)
        return
    }
    BookstoreDB.Create(&newBook)
    w.WriteHeader(http.StatusCreated)
    json.NewEncoder(w).Encode(newBook)
}
```

Once integrated, posting JSON book data to this endpoint would result in a new book record. Essential fields like title, author, and genre can be part of the submitted data.

Reading Book Details

Read operations allow users to fetch details about a book. It's akin to picking a book from a shelf and examining its cover, blurb, and author.

```go
func GetBookHandler(w http.ResponseWriter, r *http.Request) {
    vars := mux.Vars(r)
    bookID := vars["id"]
    var fetchedBook Book
    if err := BookstoreDB.First(&fetchedBook, bookID).Error; err != nil {
        http.Error(w, "Book not found", http.StatusNotFound)
        return
    }
    json.NewEncoder(w).Encode(fetchedBook)
}
```

Given a book ID, this handler retrieves and displays the respective book's details.

Updating Book

Books might undergo updates, whether it's a revised edition or updated metadata. The PUT method caters to these modifications.

```go
func UpdateBookHandler(w http.ResponseWriter, r *http.Request) {
    vars := mux.Vars(r)
    bookID := vars["id"]
    var updatedBook Book
    if err := BookstoreDB.First(&updatedBook, bookID).Error; err != nil {
        http.Error(w, "Book not found", http.StatusNotFound)
        return
    }
    decoder := json.NewDecoder(r.Body)
    err := decoder.Decode(&updatedBook)
    if err != nil {
        http.Error(w, "Invalid data", http.StatusBadRequest)
        return
    }
    BookstoreDB.Save(&updatedBook)
    w.WriteHeader(http.StatusOK)
    json.NewEncoder(w).Encode(updatedBook)
}
```

By submitting updated book data, the specified book record undergoes a transformation, mirroring the revised details.

Deleting Book

Whether it's out of stock or removed from listings, books sometimes need to be deleted from the store's database.

```go
func DeleteBookHandler(w http.ResponseWriter, r *http.Request) {
    vars := mux.Vars(r)
    bookID := vars["id"]
    var bookToDelete Book
    if err := BookstoreDB.First(&bookToDelete, bookID).Error; err != nil {
        http.Error(w, "Book not found", http.StatusNotFound)
        return
```

```
        }
        BookstoreDB.Delete(&bookToDelete)
        w.WriteHeader(http.StatusNoContent)
}
```

Invoking this endpoint with a book ID ensures the respective book's removal from the database.

Now that these CRUD operations are in place, the digital framework of the GitforGits Bookstore becomes very versatile. These handlers direct the lifecycle of each book as readers peruse the virtual aisles, from its initial upload to any updates that may be installed and finally removed. In reality, these CRUD endpoints are the lifeblood of the bookshop, not just lines of code. They make sure the store is always changing, direct user journeys, and dictate interactions.

Summary

This chapter went into great detail about one of the most important parts of making web apps: handling HTTP requests and routing them effectively. First, we gave an overview of HTTP. Next, we learned about the basic idea behind the request-response model, which is what the World Wide Web is built on. This foundation made it a lot easier to understand the beauty and complexity of web interactions, especially in the context of a web-based platform like the GitforGits Bookstore.

After getting a basic understanding of these ideas, we moved on to using handlers and handler functions by putting the net/http package into action. As the handlers for different web requests, these entities are very important in Go-based web applications. In the case of the bookstore application, the role of the application is to be a careful shopkeeper, carefully taking in customer requests (web requests) and getting the right book (web resource) in response. Routes are also the complicated paths that make these interactions possible. The bookstore was able to handle a wide range of book-related queries quickly and easily by using dynamic URL parameters.

The routing abilities were greatly improved when we used the Gorilla/Mux library. This strong library, which has features like middleware support and regex-based route matching, has made it possible to add advanced features to web applications. After that, we learned in depth about rate limiting and request throttling, two important tools for making sure servers work at their best and resources are used efficiently. These techniques watch over the GitforGits Bookstore, making sure that everyone has equal access and keeping people safe from possible dangers.

In the end, the chapter ended with an explanation of CRUD operations, which are basic parts of any data-based application. We learned how to create, access, change, and delete book records by putting what we learned into practice. This made the GitforGits Bookstore a dynamic and interactive platform. This functional part brought the bookstore back to life and helped it grow and change to meet the needs of its customers who were interested in literature. By using the lessons in this chapter, the GitforGits Bookstore's digital infrastructure has been improved and made more flexible, which has led to great experiences for users.

Chapter 4: Templating and Rendering Content

Dynamic Rendering Overview

One of the more nuanced approaches in this field is called dynamic rendering, and it enables bots to render on the server while simultaneously presenting client-side rendering to users. Users receive a version of the content that is rich in JavaScript, while search engines receive a version of the content that has already been rendered and is static. Utilizing this hybrid approach guarantees that websites are not only user-friendly but also optimized for search engines.

Historically, web pages were frequently rendered in a static manner, meaning that the content was pre-existing and could not be altered after the server response. Following that, the era of Single Page Applications (SPAs) emerged, which were accompanied by frameworks such as React and Vue. In this case, the majority of the rendering responsibility was transferred to the client side, which resulted in web pages becoming interactive but typically taking longer to paint with meaningful colors. The use of dynamic rendering allows for the best of both worlds to be achieved, ensuring that both the user experience and the discoverability of a website are optimized.

The use of dynamic rendering is a significant step forward for GitforGits Bookstore. There is a constant process of change taking place in the digital shelves of the bookstore, which are filled with a wide variety of titles, genres, and author biographies. The platform's content is constantly evolving as new books are published and older ones are taken off the shelves. When it comes to presenting this fluid content landscape to users, agility is required, and dynamic rendering excels in this regard.

Consider the scenario of a reader who is looking for a recently published fantasy novel. The dynamic rendering ensures that the information regarding the book, including reviews and the current availability status, is displayed in real time. Simultaneously, the pre-rendered version ensures that the most recent book additions are indexed promptly, making them discoverable for a wider audience. This is particularly beneficial for search engine crawlers that are responsible for scanning the website.

It is of the utmost importance for online platforms to have visibility on search engines. Although single-page applications (SPAs) offer interactive user experiences, the client-side rendering of these applications can sometimes impede search engine crawlers, which can result in less-than-ideal indexing. Dynamic rendering ensures that the vast collection of the bookstore is accurately represented in search engine results by providing these crawlers with a version that has been pre-rendered on the server side.

Alternatively, when a user visits the GitforGits Bookstore, the client-side rendering version offers a seamless and interactive browsing experience. This is the opposite end of the spectrum. Every time a user filters, searches, or explores a book, the content is dynamically reshaped to present results that are specific to that user. Because of this dynamic interactivity, users are guaranteed to find exactly what they are looking for, whether it be a best-selling thriller, a timeless romance, or a cutting-edge science fiction novella.

Platforms such as GitforGits Bookstore are a success thanks to the implementation of dynamic rendering. This increases discoverability while simultaneously providing users with experiences that are unparalleled. This is accomplished by ensuring that the platform is both search engine optimized and user-centric. As the bookstore grows and adds more literary gems from around the world, dynamic rendering makes sure it stays a beacon for book lovers around the world, always ready to offer the next great book in the best way possible. In spite of the fact that the bookstore is expanding and now houses literary treasures from all over the world, dynamic rendering guarantees that it will continue to serve as a beacon for book lovers all over the world, always prepared to provide the next great read in the most efficient manner possible.

Templates Deep Dive

Symphony of Variables

Every template engine thrives on dynamic content insertion. The beating heart of this dynamic nature is variables. In the Go template package, variables allow data to flow seamlessly from your Go code into the HTML rendering.

Each book, with its title, author, and genre, can be a variable in a template. When displaying a book page, the Go backend might send a Book struct to the template. Using {{.Title}}, {{.Author}}, or {{.Genre}} in the template would dynamically display the book's details. This is the magic of variables: they act as placeholders that the template engine replaces with actual data during rendering.

Loops

Often, web pages need to display lists of items. For the bookstore, imagine displaying a list of bestsellers. Instead of manually creating a block for each book, loops in templates come to the rescue.

In Go templates, the {{range .Books}}...{{end}} construct allows iterative rendering. Within this block, individual book details can be accessed and displayed. This mechanism is incredibly efficient. If the bookstore has a promotional week with a curated list of ten special books, the same template, without any modification, can render all of them, thanks to the power of loops.

Conditions

Sometimes, content rendering needs decisions. What if the GitforGits Bookstore wants to display a special badge for rare, collector's edition books? Conditions within templates provide this capability.

Using the {{if .IsRare}}...{{else}}...{{end}} construct, templates can make decisions. If a book is marked as a rare edition in the backend data, the condition evaluates as true, and the corresponding block within the if gets rendered. Otherwise, the else block (if provided) takes over. This conditional rendering ensures that templates remain clean and efficient, displaying content based on specific criteria.

Let us look at an example wherein the bookstore's homepage needs to display a list of trending books, but only if they have a rating above 4.5. This scenario intertwines variables, loops, and conditions. The template would first loop through the list of trending books using the range construct. Within this loop, an if condition checks each book's rating. If it's above 4.5, the template displays the book using variables like {{.Title}} and {{.Author}}.

```
{{range .TrendingBooks}}
   {{if .Rating > 4.5}}
      <h2>{{.Title}}</h2>
      <p>By {{.Author}}</p>
   {{end}}
{{end}}
```

Because of these constructs, GitforGits Bookstore is able to provide users with a seamless representation of the vast and ever-changing literary landscape. These template tools have the ability to shape the user experience in a variety of ways, including displaying the details of a rare book, iterating through a curated list of recommendations, and deciding which promotional banners to display.

Nested Templates in Action

Essentially, think of nested templates as building blocks, each fitting seamlessly within another, forming a coherent and structured whole. For GitforGits Bookstore, the utility of nested templates becomes apparent when considering the array of different sections that make up the site - headers, footers, sidebars, main content, and more. Each of these sections can be a standalone template, and when constructing a full page, these templates can be nested within a primary template. This modular approach ensures ease of updates, consistency across pages, and a unified design language.

Constructing the Framework

We shall begin by crafting a base template for the bookstore. This foundational template can have placeholders for nested templates, ensuring flexibility in content rendering.

```
{{define "base"}}
<html>
<head>
    <title>GitforGits Bookstore</title>
</head>
<body>
    {{template "header" .}}
    {{template "content" .}}
    {{template "footer" .}}
</body>
</html>
{{end}}
```

In the above snippet, "header", "content", and "footer" are the named placeholders where nested templates can be inserted.

Carving the Header

The header, often consistent across the website, can be carved into a separate template. It might contain the bookstore's logo, navigation links, and perhaps a search bar.

```
{{define "header"}}
<div class="header">
    <img src="logo.png" alt="GitforGits Logo">
    <ul class="navigation">
        <li>Home</li>
        <li>Bestsellers</li>
        <li>Genres</li>
    </ul>
</div>
{{end}}
```

Crafting the Content

The "content" placeholder is where the versatility of nested templates truly shines. Depending on the page—be it a list of bestsellers, an author's biography, or a book review—the content template can be dynamically swapped.

```
{{define "booklist"}}
<div class="book-list">
   {{range .Books}}
      <div class="book">
         <h2>{{.Title}}</h2>
         <p>By {{.Author}}</p>
      </div>
   {{end}}
</div>
{{end}}
```

Sealing the Footer

The footer, like the header, remains relatively consistent, housing information like contact details, terms of service, and social media links.

```
{{define "footer"}}
<div class="footer">
   <p>Contact us at contact@gitforgits.com</p>
   <ul class="social-media">
      <li>Facebook</li>
      <li>Twitter</li>
   </ul>
</div>
{{end}}
```

To construct a complete webpage, these nested templates can be rendered within the base template. Using Go's template execution functions, specific content templates (like "booklist") can be injected into the base, forming a complete, structured webpage.

Design Main Page Layout

The main page of any website is akin to a storefront. For GitforGits Bookstore, it's the virtual entrance, inviting users to explore the vast literary treasures within. It should not only showcase the variety but also offer a glimpse into special features, like bestsellers, new arrivals, and user reviews. This is where design meets functionality, ensuring a compelling and seamless browsing

experience.
Structuring Base Layout
To get started, try visualizing the components that make up the main page's structure. Imagine the layout of a website that includes a prominent header that contains links to navigation, a dynamic content area that displays books, and a footer that contains essential information about the website. Each of these components can be crafted as a separate template, which enables modular design and reusability of the product.

```
{{define "base"}}
<html>
<head>
   <title>GitforGits Bookstore: Home</title>
</head>
<body>
   {{template "header" .}}
   {{template "mainContent" .}}
   {{template "footer" .}}
</body>
</html>
{{end}}
```

Designing Header
The header should be both visually appealing and functionally efficient. It needs to house the brand logo, primary navigation links, and potentially a search bar for users to find specific titles.

```
{{define "header"}}
<div class="header">
   <img src="logo.png" alt="GitforGits Logo">
   <ul class="navigation">
      <li>Home</li>
      <li>Bestsellers</li>
      <li>New Arrivals</li>
      <li>Genres</li>
   </ul>
   <div class="search">
```

```
      <input type="text" placeholder="Search for books...">
      <button>Search</button>
    </div>
</div>
{{end}}
```

Building Dynamic Content Area
The primary section of the main page is where the magic happens. Books can be categorized into different sections like 'Featured', 'Bestsellers', or 'User Recommendations'. For each category, a loop can iterate through a list of books, displaying them dynamically.

```
{{define "mainContent"}}
<div class="content">

    <section class="featured">
        <h2>Featured Books</h2>
        {{range .FeaturedBooks}}
            <div class="book">
                <img src="{{.ImageURL}}" alt="{{.Title}}">
                <h3>{{.Title}}</h3>
                <p>By {{.Author}}</p>
            </div>
        {{end}}
    </section>

    <section class="bestsellers">
        <h2>Bestsellers</h2>
        {{range .BestsellingBooks}}
            <div class="book">
                <img src="{{.ImageURL}}" alt="{{.Title}}">
                <h3>{{.Title}}</h3>
                <p>By {{.Author}}</p>
            </div>
        {{end}}
```

```
      </section>

      <section class="recommendations">
        <h2>User Recommendations</h2>
        {{range .UserRecommended}}
          <div class="book">
            <img src="{{.ImageURL}}" alt="{{.Title}}">
            <h3>{{.Title}}</h3>
            <p>By {{.Author}}</p>
          </div>
        {{end}}
      </section>

</div>
{{end}}
```

Outlining Holistic Footer

The footer rounds off the main page by providing essential links, contact information, and social media connectivity. It ensures users have access to necessary resources, irrespective of where they are on the page.

```
{{define "footer"}}
<div class="footer">
   <ul>
      <li>About Us</li>
      <li>Contact</li>
      <li>Terms of Service</li>
   </ul>
   <div class="social-icons">
      <img src="facebook-icon.png">
      <img src="twitter-icon.png">
   </div>
   <p>&copy; 2023 GitforGits Bookstore</p>
</div>
```

{{end}}

This modular approach ensures each section gets the attention it deserves. From the welcoming embrace of the header to the diverse literary showcase in the main content, down to the resource-rich footer, every pixel is meticulously crafted.

Handling Forms and User Inputs

A web application's capacity to receive and process user inputs is fundamental to its interactive nature. In order to facilitate this interaction, forms serve as bridges that enable users to submit data. This data can be used for a variety of purposes, including registering for an account, providing feedback, or placing an order. It is anticipated that forms will play a significant part in the process of capturing user preferences, orders, and reviews for the GitforGits Bookstore.

Laying Groundwork

Web forms are primarily created using the HTML <form> element. Within this, various input elements, such as text fields (<input>), checkboxes, radio buttons, and dropdown lists, capture data. The data entered into these fields gets sent to the server when the form is submitted.

Consider a user registration form for the bookstore. Such a form would capture essential details like username, email, password, and perhaps, user preferences. Given below is how it might look:

```html
<form action="/register" method="post">
    <label for="username">Username:</label>
    <input type="text" id="username" name="username">

    <label for="email">Email:</label>
    <input type="email" id="email" name="email">

    <label for="password">Password:</label>
    <input type="password" id="password" name="password">

    <input type="submit" value="Register">
</form>
```

Dropdowns, Radios, and Checkboxes

Beyond simple text inputs, forms can contain elements that allow users to make selections. Suppose the GitforGits Bookstore offers a feature for users to set preferences regarding genres they're interested in. Dropdowns, radios, and checkboxes would be apt choices.

```
<label for="favGenre">Favorite Genre:</label>
<select id="favGenre" name="favGenre">
   <option value="fiction">Fiction</option>
   <option value="non-fiction">Non-Fiction</option>
   <option value="sci-fi">Science Fiction</option>
</select>

<label>Preferred Authors:</label>
<input type="checkbox" id="author1" name="author1" value="Author One">
<label for="author1">Author One</label>

<input type="checkbox" id="author2" name="author2" value="Author Two">
<label for="author2">Author Two</label>
```

Validation

Ensuring that users provide valid input is paramount. HTML5 offers built-in validation features like required fields and pattern matching. For instance, the email input type will check for a valid email format. Adding a required attribute will ensure that a field is not left empty.

```
<input type="email" id="email" name="email" required>
```

Processing Form Data

Once a form is submitted, the server needs to process the input data. With Go, the net/http package makes this task straightforward. The Request object contains form data which can be easily parsed and processed.

Now, once the registration form is submitted, the server can extract the form data using:

```
username := r.FormValue("username")
email := r.FormValue("email")
password := r.FormValue("password")
```

The addition of forms to GitforGits Bookstore enhances its interactivity and user-centric approach. It is guaranteed that the user will always feel heard, that their preferences will be honored, and that their data will be secure thanks to the dialogue that is initiated through forms and is supported by the processing power of Go.

Template Caching

Overview

Imagine going to GitforGits and finding that the store's layout is completely rearranged with each page you turn to. Infuriating, don't you think? A phenomenon that is analogous to this one occurs in modern web applications due to the fact that templates are parsed and loaded from scratch for each and every user request. Not only does it result in a waste of computational resources, but it also causes lag, which in turn reduces the quality of the user experience. For the purposes of this learnings, template caching is comparable to the process of establishing a stable floor plan in a physical store, which guarantees uniformity and facilitates quick navigation for each and every customer.

A straightforward explanation of template caching is that it involves storing pre-parsed templates in memory. This makes them readily available for subsequent requests without the need for reparsing, which is an overhead. The response times of the server are significantly improved by this mechanism, which guarantees that the end user will receive content in a timely manner.

Go's Template Package

Go's html/template package is adept at parsing and storing templates. Typically, when rendering a response, one might use template.ParseFiles() or template.ParseGlob() on-the-fly. While effective, it's computationally intensive if repeated for every request. Instead of parsing templates within handler functions, the parsing can be performed at application startup. By doing so, a cache of parsed templates is created, held in memory, and readily available for use.

```go
var templateCache = template.New("").Delims("{{", "}}")

func LoadTemplates() {
    templates, err := templateCache.ParseGlob("./templates/*.gohtml")
    if err != nil {
        log.Fatal(err)
    }
    templateCache = templates
}
```

In this snippet, the LoadTemplates function populates the global templateCache with parsed templates. By invoking this function at application start, the parsed templates become readily accessible throughout the application's lifecycle.

Deploying Cached Templates

With the cache in place, rendering a response becomes a streamlined process. Suppose a user accesses a book listing on GitforGits:

```go
func BookListHandler(w http.ResponseWriter, r *http.Request) {
    books := fetchBooks()
    err := templateCache.ExecuteTemplate(w, "booklist.gohtml", books)
    if err != nil {
        http.Error(w, "Internal Server Error", http.StatusInternalServerError)
    }
}
```

In the BookListHandler, instead of parsing the template anew, the handler directly taps into the templateCache, swiftly serving the request using the pre-parsed "booklist.gohtml" template.

The outcomes of template caching are multi-fold:
- By eliminating the overhead of parsing, response times get a significant boost.
- Reducing redundant operations ensures efficient CPU utilization.
- Using a centralized cache prevents potential inconsistencies that might arise from parsing templates in various parts of an application.

However, while caching enhances production performance, during the development phase, it might obscure changes made to templates since the cache retains the initially parsed versions. Developers must refresh the cache to visualize updates.

Safe HTML Rendering
Need for Safe Rendering

The need for safe rendering in web applications is paramount, especially in platforms that thrive on user interactivity and content submission. For GitforGits Bookstore, users might have the ability to submit reviews or comments on books. This feature greatly enhances user engagement and community building but simultaneously opens up avenues for security vulnerabilities, particularly from malicious users who might inject harmful scripts into their submissions. Safe HTML rendering is thus essential to ensure that user-submitted content is displayed securely, without compromising the integrity, security, or functionality of the web application.

Cross-Site Scripting (XSS)

One of the most prevalent threats in this context is Cross-Site Scripting (XSS), where attackers embed harmful scripts into content that is then served to other users. This type of attack can have serious implications. For example, in GitforGits Bookstore, if an attacker submits a book review containing a malicious script, any user who views this review could inadvertently execute the script. This could lead to various malicious outcomes, such as data theft, session hijacking, or the spreading of malware. The risk is particularly high because the harmful script appears in a trusted context – the bookstore website – making users less likely to suspect foul play.

Contextual Encoding

To combat such threats, it is crucial to employ robust measures like contextual encoding. The html/template package in Go is a prime example of a tool designed for safe rendering. It automatically escapes user input based on its context, a crucial feature for preventing XSS attacks. For instance, if user data is placed within a script tag, the package treats it as data rather than executable script. This automatic escaping extends to various contexts, including HTML attributes, JavaScript, URLs, and CSS. Such contextual awareness in encoding ensures that user-submitted content is rendered safely, mitigating the risk of malicious code execution.

For example, rendering the following in a template:

```
{{.UserReview}}
```

If UserReview contains harmful scripts, Go's templating system would escape it appropriately, rendering the script harmless.

In rare cases, you might trust the source of the HTML and want to render it without escaping. Go's html/template provides a mechanism for this with the template.HTML type. However, caution is paramount when using this, as it exposes the application to potential XSS attacks.

```
trustedHTML := template.HTML(userGeneratedHTML)
```

This informs Go that the HTML content should be rendered as-is, without automatic escaping. It's crucial to use this only when you're certain of the HTML's safety.

Apart from HTML, web applications often deal with other types of content. GitforGits might have dynamic CSS for themes or user-customizable JavaScript features. Go's templating system provides types like template.JS, template.URL, and template.CSS to safely render these content types.

For instance, to safely embed user-generated JavaScript:

```
trustedJS := template.JS(userGeneratedJS)
```

While Go offers robust safety mechanisms, manual validation and sanitization remain crucial. Before rendering user-generated content, even with automatic escaping, validate the input. Check for appropriate content length, ensure it adheres to expected formats, and strip out or neutralize any potentially harmful content.

Template Debugging

Bugs, including those that are present in templates, are unavoidable, regardless of the level of expertise present in a developer. Keeping the user experience as smooth as possible is of the utmost importance for GitforGits Bookstore, so it is imperative that templates render correctly. The ability to quickly identify and correct template-related anomalies is a skill that can be acquired by developers through the study of debugging techniques and the comprehension of common error scenarios.

Go's html/template package, while powerful, can present errors due to various reasons such as malformed templates, missing data, or incorrect template logic. Grasping the common culprits can expedite the debugging process.

Scenario#1: Malformed Templates

Suppose, in your excitement to showcase a new book release, you draft a template but mistakenly introduce a syntax error:

```
{{if .IsNewRelease}
   <p>New Release!</p>
{{end}}
```

The missing closing parenthesis after .IsNewRelease will cause a parse error.

Debugging Approach
- Whenever a template fails to parse, Go will return an error. Always check for errors when parsing templates.
- The error message will provide a clue. In this case, it might say something about a mismatched or missing delimiter.
- Scan the template for any syntactical discrepancies, especially around the area highlighted by the error.

Scenario#2: Missing or Mismatched Data

Imagine you're rendering user reviews, but accidentally reference a non-existent field:

`{{.UserRevu}} <!-- Typo in the field name -->`

Debugging Approach
- Errors related to missing data will emerge at runtime when executing the template, not during parsing.
- Cross-reference the template's placeholders with the data structure it's expected to represent.
- Ensure there aren't any typos or mismatches between the data field names and their references in the template.

Scenario#3: Incorrect Logic or Conditions

Suppose you're offering discounts on certain books, and your template contains logic to showcase the discount:

```
{{if .Discount > 50}}
    <p>Major Discount!</p>
{{else}}
    <p>Regular Price</p>
{{end}}
```

However, you forgot that Discount is a string representing a percentage, not an integer.

Debugging Approach
- This scenario might not throw a direct error. Instead, it may lead to unexpected behavior, like showing "Regular Price" for a 60% discount.
- Thoroughly review any template logic or conditions. Ensure data types and conditions align with expectations.
- Consider introducing unit tests or template tests. For GitforGits Bookstore, having tests for critical template logic ensures they render as expected under different data conditions.
- Apart from manual checks, tools can be indispensable:
- Go Playground: For basic templates, Go's online playground can be useful to test and debug templates in isolation.
- Custom Error Wrappers: Consider writing a custom wrapper around the template.Execute() method. This wrapper can capture errors and provide additional

context, making debugging more straightforward.

Summary

In this chapter, we explored the intricate process of web rendering using Go's templating system. We emphasized the importance of delivering dynamic content for GitforGits Bookstore. The chapter delves into the concept of dynamic rendering and emphasizes the transition from static web pages to interactive and dynamic user experiences. Go templates make this transformation possible by allowing developers to create pages that adapt to user data, application states, or other dynamic variables.

Further, the chapter delves into the complexities of Go's templating syntax, including fundamental elements such as variables, loops, and conditions. These essential components animate web pages, allowing them to respond and adjust to data in real time. The addition of nested templates, a powerful feature, demonstrated the efficient construction of more complex web pages by assembling various template components. The GitforGits Bookstore's learning process was made more practical and relatable by applying each concept in a hands-on manner within a real-world context.

The second section of the chapter emphasized the importance of safety, specifically learning potential flaws related to user-generated content. The ability of Go to securely process HTML was demonstrated, providing protection against common vulnerabilities such as Cross-Site Scripting (XSS). A proactive strategy that prioritized manual validation and vigilant content monitoring, in addition to automated defenses, was advocated for in the chapter. The chapter concluded with a learning of the much-feared subject of debugging. By presenting various scenarios, readers were given strategies for detecting and correcting common template errors, ensuring the smooth operation of the GitforGits platform.

Chapter 5: Interaction with Databases

Introduction to Persistent Storage

Data is central to most web applications. Data drives functionality and user experience, whether it's user profiles, order histories, or product catalogs. However, for data to truly serve its purpose, it requires a dependable storage mechanism that keeps information longer than the ephemeral lifecycle of a single server instance or user session. This is where persistent storage comes into play, providing a long-term, stable repository for data that underpins the core functions of the application.

While the primary function of persistent storage is to protect data, the implications are numerous. It allows for features such as user personalization, order tracking, and product recommendations. This means remembering a user's reading preferences, bookmarking their last read page, and suggesting books based on their reading history for GitforGits Bookstore. Every interaction with the website would be stateless, devoid of history or context, severely limiting the depth of user engagement.

Databases inevitably take center stage when learning persistent storage. They not only store data but also provide structured methods for querying, retrieving, and manipulating it. Relational databases, such as PostgreSQL or MySQL, and NoSQL databases, such as MongoDB, are two types of databases. The database of choice is frequently determined by the application's specific requirements. For example, an inventory-centric application such as GitforGits Bookstore may favor relational databases due to their structured nature, which allows for complex queries on book titles, authors, genres, and user reviews.

Drivers or libraries that translate high-level programming logic into database-specific commands are used by web applications to communicate with databases. This could include leveraging the database/sql package, as well as drivers specific to the chosen database, in the context of GitforGits developed in Go. A web application's relationship with its database is delicate; efficient data retrieval and storage mechanisms have a direct impact on the application's performance, scalability, and user experience.

As the number of web applications increases, so does the volume of data. GitforGits Bookstore may host millions of books and serve thousands of concurrent users over time. Traditional databases may experience strain under such conditions, resulting in slower response times. Enter modern solutions such as distributed databases, caching mechanisms, and database sharding, all of which aim to scale persistent storage to meet escalating demands without losing performance.

Persistent storage isn't just a backend concern for a web application; it's the lifeline that ensures continuity, context, and personalization. It remembers returning users, remembers their preferences, and creates tailored experiences for them. It's the difference between a static online book catalog and a dynamic literary haven that evolves, learns, and grows alongside its readers. It is the unsung hero who works behind the scenes to make modern web experiences not only possible, but exceptional.

database/sql Package

Overview

Go offers an in-built package named database/sql for working with relational databases. It's a generic interface, meaning it can be used with a variety of relational databases such as PostgreSQL, MySQL, or SQLite. For the GitforGits Bookstore, it can serve as a powerful tool to manage book inventories, user accounts, transactions, and reviews. Unlike ORMs, which abstract away most of the database interactions, database/sql provides a balance between abstraction and control, offering both simplicity and fine-grained control over database operations.

Install Drivers

The database/sql package operates in tandem with specific drivers for each database. A driver interprets generic SQL commands into instructions comprehensible by the specific database in use. Before delving into the package's functionality, it's imperative to choose and install an appropriate driver. Let us assume we're using PostgreSQL for GitforGits:

```
go get -u github.com/lib/pq
```

With the driver in place, we can now proceed to establish connections and interact with the database.

Connecting Database

Using the sql.Open() function, we can initiate this connection:

```go
import (
   "database/sql"
   _ "github.com/lib/pq"
)

func main() {
   connStr := "user=username dbname=gitforgits_bookstore password=password host=localhost sslmode=disable"
   db, err := sql.Open("postgres", connStr)
   if err != nil {
      log.Fatal(err)
```

```
    }
    defer db.Close()
}
```

Do not forget the use of an underscore _ when importing the pq driver. This ensures the driver registers itself with the database/sql package without adding any other bloat to the namespace.

Crafting and Executing Queries

With a connection established, you can begin crafting SQL queries for the bookstore. For instance, to retrieve a list of books:

```
rows, err := db.Query("SELECT title, author FROM books")
if err != nil {
    log.Fatal(err)
}
defer rows.Close()

for rows.Next() {
    var title, author string
    if err := rows.Scan(&title, &author); err != nil {
        log.Fatal(err)
    }
    fmt.Printf("Title: %s, Author: %s\n", title, author)
}
```

Insertions, Updates, and Deletions

Modifying the database involves using the Exec method:

```
result, err := db.Exec("INSERT INTO books (title, author) VALUES ($1, $2)", "Go Programming", "Jane Doe")
if err != nil {
    log.Fatal(err)
}
```

This method can be used for updates and deletions, as well. For operations that modify the database, it's often crucial to handle transactional integrity. The database/sql package offers transaction methods like Begin, Commit, and Rollback to ensure operations are atomic.

Managing Database Connections

The database/sql package internally manages a pool of connections. However, you can set parameters like maximum open connections or maximum idle connections:

db.SetMaxOpenConns(10)
db.SetMaxIdleConns(3)

Through the database/sql package, GitforGits Bookstore gains the capability to weave intricate relationships with its data. Whether it's cataloging a new collection, recalling a user's favorite genre, or processing a transaction, every interaction is seamlessly underpinned by a robust database connection.

Sample Program: Design Robust Database

Nature of Data

The heart of the GitforGits Bookstore is, undoubtedly, its vast collection of books. However, a closer look reveals intricate interrelations between various data entities: users, their reading habits, book genres, reviews, and more. A meticulously designed database schema ensures that the application not only stores data but captures the rich tapestry of relationships, interactions, and dynamics.

Books as Core Entity

The central table in our schema will be books. Each book has unique attributes and can be associated with multiple categories, reviews, and transactions.

```
CREATE TABLE books (
    id SERIAL PRIMARY KEY,
    title VARCHAR(255) NOT NULL,
    author VARCHAR(255) NOT NULL,
    isbn VARCHAR(13),
    description TEXT,
    publication_date DATE,
    genre_id INT,
    price DECIMAL(10,2)
```

);

This structure captures essential details of a book. The genre_id is a foreign key, hinting at another table that catalogs genres.

Categorizing Books as Genres

Diverse genres help readers navigate the bookstore and find books of their interest.

CREATE TABLE genres (
   id SERIAL PRIMARY KEY,
   name VARCHAR(100) UNIQUE NOT NULL
);

This straightforward table lists genres, linking back to books via the genre_id foreign key.

Users

A bookstore is incomplete without its patrons. The users table manages user data and their interactions with the store.

CREATE TABLE users (
   id SERIAL PRIMARY KEY,
   username VARCHAR(255) UNIQUE NOT NULL,
   email VARCHAR(255) UNIQUE NOT NULL,
   password_hash CHAR(64) NOT NULL,
   signup_date DATE DEFAULT CURRENT_DATE
);

The password_hash column indicates a hash of the user's password, adhering to best security practices.

Book Reviews

Users can pen down their feelings about books in reviews.

CREATE TABLE reviews (
   id SERIAL PRIMARY KEY,

```
    user_id INT REFERENCES users(id),
    book_id INT REFERENCES books(id),
    rating INT CHECK (rating >= 1 AND rating <= 5),
    comment TEXT,
    review_date DATE DEFAULT CURRENT_DATE
);
```

This schema captures the review, the associated user, and book, ensuring every opinion finds its rightful place in the ecosystem.

Transactions

When users buy books, the transactions need tracking. Transactions tie a user to a book, signifying a successful sale.

```
CREATE TABLE transactions (
    id SERIAL PRIMARY KEY,
    user_id INT REFERENCES users(id),
    book_id INT REFERENCES books(id),
    purchase_date DATE DEFAULT CURRENT_DATE,
    amount DECIMAL(10,2)
);
```

Inventory Management

To ensure books are in stock, an inventory table is essential.

```
CREATE TABLE inventory (
    book_id INT REFERENCES books(id),
    stock_quantity INT NOT NULL,
    restock_threshold INT,
    last_restock_date DATE
);
```

This schema aids in tracking stock levels and can trigger restock alerts when quantities dip below the threshold. The proposed schema ensures every detail, every transaction, and every review is captured, processed, and presented, ensuring the bookstore's operations are smooth, efficient, and insightful.

Leverage ORMs

While direct SQL queries provide the utmost control over database operations, they can also become cumbersome, especially as an application scales. Object-Relational Mapping (ORM) tools bridge the gap between the object-oriented paradigm of programming languages and the relational nature of databases. Instead of writing SQL queries, developers interact with their data as objects. For the GitforGits Bookstore, using an ORM could mean dealing with Book, User, or Review objects directly, making code more intuitive and maintainable. ORMs comprehensive features, combined with its seamless integration with Go, make it an excellent choice for the GitforGits Bookstore. Features include automatic migrations, associations, hooks, and more. By using GORM, you abstract away the SQL layer, allowing you to focus on business logic rather than intricate SQL queries.

One of the significant advantages of using an ORM like GORM is rapid application development. By abstracting away the SQL, developers can quickly scaffold out functionalities. For the GitforGits Bookstore, this means faster development cycles for features like adding books, user registration, or processing transactions. This speed doesn't sacrifice the flexibility, as GORM allows for raw SQL queries when needed.

With ORMs, there's less room for SQL errors as the tool generates queries based on defined models. For GitforGits, it ensures database interactions remain consistent. Whether it's retrieving a book or updating user details, the operations follow the same underlying patterns, ensuring a uniformity in data operations.

For GitforGits Bookstore, relationships between entities like books, users, and reviews are pivotal. ORMs shine here. With GORM, setting up a one-to-many or many-to-many relationship is straightforward. For instance, associating multiple reviews with a book or associating multiple book purchases with a user becomes an intuitive task. As the GitforGits Bookstore evolves, its database schema will need updates. ORMs, especially GORM, offer automatic migrations. Instead of manually crafting ALTER queries, you simply update your Go models, and the ORM adjusts the underlying database structure accordingly.

Advanced ORMs provide middleware and hooks, allowing developers to tap into the lifecycle of data operations. For GitforGits, it could mean validating a new user's data before it's saved or modifying a book's details before an update operation. These hooks ensure data integrity and allow for advanced functionalities without the added complexity of manual SQL triggers or procedures.

Strengthen Database Indexing

Database indexing is a critical aspect of database management, akin to the index found in a book. Just as a book's index allows readers to quickly locate specific information without flipping through every page, a database index enhances the speed and efficiency of data retrieval by eliminating the need to scan each row in a table. This is particularly vital for applications like GitforGits Bookstore, which likely deals with a substantial and ever-expanding volume of data. Efficient indexing in such a context means that when a user searches for a book, the system can swiftly locate and retrieve the relevant information from a vast repository, rather than laboriously combing through every single entry. This not only applies to book searches but also extends to rapidly accessing user profiles, transaction records, and other pertinent data. The importance of this cannot be overstated, especially as the bookstore grows in both its inventory and user base. Proper indexing ensures that the application remains responsive and efficient, providing a seamless experience for users who expect quick and accurate search results, whether they are browsing for books, checking their user accounts, or reviewing past transactions.

It is also crucial to understand the different types of indexes, primary and secondary indexing, as both play pivotal roles in database management and query optimization.

Primary Indexing

Primary indexing is associated with the primary key of a database table. A primary key is a unique identifier for each record in the table, such as a book's unique ID in the GitforGits Bookstore database. The primary index is automatically created when the primary key is defined. This index is crucial for quickly locating records when queries are made using the primary key. For instance, when a user searches for a book using its unique ID, the primary index allows the database to quickly locate and retrieve that specific book's data without scanning the entire table.

Secondary Indexing

Secondary indexing, on the other hand, involves creating indexes on columns other than the primary key. These are particularly useful for speeding up queries that involve non-primary key columns. For example, in GitforGits Bookstore, users might want to search for books by author, genre, or publication date. Secondary indexes on these columns would significantly enhance the speed of these searches. Unlike primary indexes, secondary indexes are not automatically created and must be defined based on the query patterns and requirements of the application.

Primary vs. Secondary Indexes

While primary keys inherently come indexed, secondary indexes need to be explicitly defined. In the context of GitforGits, the id columns of tables like books, users, and reviews have primary indexes. However, scenarios where searches happen on non-primary key columns, like searching books by title or isbn, necessitate secondary indexes.

CREATE INDEX idx_books_title ON books(title);

This command establishes an index on the title column, expediting search operations centered around book titles.

Composite Indexes

Queries often involve multiple columns. For example, one might want to retrieve all books of a specific genre published after a certain date. A composite index, indexing both the genre_id and publication_date columns, enhances such queries.

CREATE INDEX idx_books_genre_date ON books(genre_id, publication_date);

For GitforGits, anticipating the nature of queries and creating composite indexes accordingly can drastically improve performance.

Covering Indexes

Covering indexes elevates optimization by including all the columns a query needs within the index itself. Suppose GitforGits often queries book titles and their respective authors. A covering index on both title and author columns would not just speed up the search but also retrieve the necessary data directly from the index.

CREATE INDEX idx_books_title_author ON books(title, author);

With this index, searches for specific titles and authors bypass the table entirely, drawing data from the index, making retrievals exceedingly fast.

Partial Indexes

Not all data requires indexing. If GitforGits, for instance, frequently searches for books priced above a certain range, a partial index can be set up:

CREATE INDEX idx_books_high_price ON books(price) WHERE price > 50;

Such an index optimizes searches for high-priced books while conserving space by not indexing lower-priced ones. For GitforGits, where new books get added or prices change, this overhead can impact performance. Hence, it's crucial to strike a balance – index columns that significantly boost search performance but be judicious to avoid over-indexing.

Manage Database Connections

Connection Pooling

The connections to databases are a resource that is both limited and expensive. Despite the fact that an application is capable of initiating multiple connections, each connection requires memory and CPU resources from both the application and the database server. If each request resulted in the establishment of a new connection, the GitforGits Bookstore would be subject to performance bottlenecks. On the other hand, connection pooling becomes the most important alternative to this expensive open-and-close approach.

The term "connection pooling" refers to a method in which a number of previously established connections are maintained in order to make them available for use in response to future requests. Imagine that you have a fleet of taxi cabs that are all set up and waiting for you. It is not necessary to have to call for a taxi each time because there is already one available. As a result, there is no waiting time required to establish a connection for GitforGits; a connection that is ready to use is made available for each and every user request, which guarantees that database interactions are fast.

Integrating Connection Pooling

There is an inherent support for connection pooling within the database/sql package of Go. Once a connection to the database has been established by using the sql.Open() function, Go will manage a pool of connections underneath it.

```
db, err := sql.Open("postgres", "connection_string_here")
if err != nil {
    log.Fatal(err)
}
```

While this initiates the connection pool, it's essential to configure it to match the application's needs.

Tuning Connection Pool

There are primary settings, GitforGits should consider as below:
- MaxOpenConns: This defines the maximum number of open connections to the database.

```
db.SetMaxOpenConns(100)
```

- MaxIdleConns: Determines the maximum number of idle connections retained in the pool.

db.SetMaxIdleConns(50)

- ConnMaxLifetime: Establishes the maximum duration a connection can be reused.

db.SetConnMaxLifetime(time.Minute * 5)

These settings should be tuned based on the GitforGits Bookstore's traffic patterns and database server capacity. Regular monitoring and adjustments helps us or ensures us that the connection pool remains optimized for the evolving needs of the application.

Connection Health Checks

Having a pool is not enough; the connections that are made within it must be in good health. It is possible for a database connection to become obsolete or to shut down entirely in certain circumstances. In order for GitforGits to function, it is essential that all connections in the pool be active and in good health. It is possible to ensure the robustness of the pool by performing regular pings on the database and validating connections.

err = db.Ping()
if err != nil {
    log.Fatal("Failed to connect to the database:", err)
}

Despite best efforts, connections can occasionally fail. The GitforGits Bookstore should have mechanisms to gracefully handle these failures. Retrying a failed connection, implementing exponential backoffs, or diverting traffic to a backup database are strategies to ensure uninterrupted service.

Advanced SQL Queries
Joins

In relational databases, joins play a crucial role because they make it possible to retrieve data from multiple tables based on relational keys. Consider a scenario in which every book found in the GitforGits Bookstore is associated with both an author and a genre. Although the tables for books, authors, and genres each contain their own distinct data, joins are able to help consolidate this data in order to produce more comprehensive outputs.

INNER JOIN

This retrieves records that have matching values in both tables. To list all books with their authors:

SELECT books.title, authors.name
FROM books
INNER JOIN authors ON books.author_id = authors.id;

LEFT JOIN

It fetches all records from the left table and matched records from the right table. To list all genres and any associated books:

SELECT genres.name, books.title
FROM genres
LEFT JOIN books ON genres.id = books.genre_id;

Subqueries

Nested queries, also known as subqueries, enable multiple retrieval steps to be performed within a single query. Imagine that GitforGits is interested in determining which author has written the most books and wants to do so:

SELECT author_id, COUNT(*) as book_count
FROM books
GROUP BY author_id
HAVING COUNT(*) = (
    SELECT MAX(book_count)
    FROM (SELECT author_id, COUNT(*) as book_count FROM books GROUP BY author_id) as counts
);

In the above, the inner query counts books per author, and the outer query identifies the author with the most books.

Aggregations

The purpose of aggregation functions is to process multiple rows of data and then compile the extracted information into a single, summarized result that offers valuable insights. Through the use of aggregations, GitforGits is able to gain a better understanding of customer behavior, monitor trends in sales, and even perform inventory management.

An example of an aggregation function would be one that determines the total number of books sold, the average price of books, or the authors or genres that are the most popular. It is essential for the GitforGits team to have these summarized results in order to make educated decisions, formulate marketing strategies, or tailor the inventory in order to more effectively meet the demands of the customers.

COUNT
Calculates the number of rows. To determine the total number of books:

SELECT COUNT(*) FROM books;

SUM
Computes the sum of values. If GitforGits wanted to know the total stock for a particular book:

SELECT SUM(stock) FROM inventory WHERE book_id = some_book_id;

AVG
Calculates the average of values. To find the average book price:

SELECT AVG(price) FROM books;

MAX & MIN
Identify the highest and lowest value, respectively. To find the most and least expensive book:

SELECT MAX(price), MIN(price) FROM books;

GROUP BY
Organizes rows sharing a property into summary rows. If GitforGits wished to list the number of books by each author:

SELECT author_id, COUNT(*) FROM books GROUP BY author_id;

HAVING
A filter applied after aggregation. To list authors who've written more than five books:

```sql
SELECT author_id, COUNT(*)
FROM books
GROUP BY author_id
HAVING COUNT(*) > 5;
```

The aforementioned advanced SQL queries teach you how to efficiently retrieve, analyze, and display database data. By learning these joins, subqueries, and aggregations, you can make complex views of data, gain deep insights, and easily meet the needs of complex users. A sturdy bridge between raw data and actionable insights. This bridge can be used for a variety of purposes, including the generation of sales reports, the recommendation of books based on complex criteria, and the provision of analytics to authors regarding their readership.

Summary

This chapter delves deeply into the world of databases, with a focus on the complexities of SQL operations that power the GitforGits Bookstore's functionality. Starting with a fundamental understanding of persistent storage, we recognized its critical importance in data preservation and application functionality. The database/sql package in Go was emphasized because it provides a powerful interface for interacting with relational databases.

We discovered the effectiveness of Joins - a mechanism that allows the integration of data from multiple tables - while investigating advanced SQL operations. We learned about different types of joins, like INNER JOIN and LEFT JOIN, and demonstrated their practical applications with real-world examples from the bookstore. Subqueries were later introduced, revealing their ability to execute nested queries for intricate data retrieval. We have enhanced our application's capabilities to conduct complex data analysis and generate results that cannot be accomplished by a single query by understanding subqueries.

Aggregations, which are fundamental to data analysis, were thoroughly investigated. We discovered the capability of converting unprocessed data into significant observations by using functions such as COUNT, SUM, AVG, MAX, MIN, GROUP BY, and HAVING. The practical situations associated with the GitforGits Bookstore demonstrated the importance of these functions, whether in producing sales summaries, managing inventory, or providing personalized user experiences. The advanced SQL techniques described in this chapter allow the GitforGits platform to provide a comprehensive, efficient, and user-centric experience. These methods ensure that data is not only saved but also effectively used to drive operations and growth.

Chapter 6: Concurrency in Go

Age of Rapid Applications

Users' patience has taken a significant hit in this age of digital technology. The demand for instant gratification is at an all-time high, thanks to the widespread availability of high-speed internet and the progression of technology from generation to generation. According to the findings of a study conducted by Google, even a delay of a few hundred milliseconds can result in a decrease in the level of user engagement. When it comes to web platforms, such as the GitforGits Bookstore, every single second that a page takes to load, a query takes to execute, or a transaction takes to finish is significant. Not only does a slow application make the user experience less enjoyable, but it also has an impact on how consumers perceive the brand, how much trust they have in it, and ultimately, how much money it brings in. Furthermore, in this day and age, where many options are available with just a click of the mouse, speed becomes a competitive advantage.

Concurrency for Parallel Execution

There are a number of factors that contribute to the speed of an application; however, one of the most important aspects is how the application manages multiple tasks effectively. The traditional method of application execution consisted of sequential tasks, which, despite being straightforward, required a significant amount of time. We shall learn about concurrency, which is the idea of carrying out multiple tasks in overlapping time periods, not necessarily at the same time. Comparable to a chef who begins preparing another dish while the first one is simmering, this situation is similar. Even though the chef is still working on one thing at a time, the tasks are beginning to overlap with one another.

Go's Concurrency Paradigm

Since its inception, Go has embraced concurrency as a fundamental principle, rather than treating it as an afterthought or an additional feature. The Go runtime is responsible for managing lightweight threads known as goroutines, which are at the core of the concurrency model used by Go. Goroutines, in contrast to traditional heavyweight threads, are inexpensive to create, have a small memory footprint, and are efficiently scheduled by Go's runtime. Consider the possibility that the GitforGits Bookstore could accommodate thousands of customers while only requiring a small number of traditional threads to handle the workload.

```
go func() {
    // concurrent function here
}()
```

With just the 'go' keyword, a function runs concurrently, allowing the GitforGits Bookstore to handle multiple user requests or database transactions seamlessly. But, with great power comes great responsibility. Managing data safely between these Goroutines becomes essential. Go provides Channels, a powerful mechanism to safely communicate and share data between

Goroutines.

```go
ch := make(chan int)
go func() {
    ch <- doSomething()  // Send data to channel
}()
value := <-ch  // Receive data from channel
```

Many programming languages offer concurrency mechanisms, but Go's approach is distinctive in its simplicity and effectiveness. Instead of relying on complex locking mechanisms, Go promotes a "share by communicating" philosophy. The synergy between Goroutines and Channels enables the development of concurrent applications with fewer bugs, less complexity, and better performance. Go's concurrency is a strong tangible benefit including faster page loads, real-time data updates, swift transaction processing, and the capability to scale for thousands of users without breaking a sweat.

Go's Goroutines

Understanding Goroutines

Go's approach to threading is called goroutines, and it has a lower overhead than threading. Additionally, they are fundamental building blocks that make it possible for functions to run simultaneously. Considering the fact that they are relatively lightweight, it is possible to generate thousands or even millions of Goroutines without causing a significant burden on the system. This lightweight quality is a result of the design of Go, which does not directly bind Goroutines to threads but instead enables the Go runtime to manage them in an effective manner.

Goroutines have the potential to be a game-changer for GitforGits Bookstore thanks to their ability to handle multiple user requests, database operations, and possibly even some background tasks such as prediction engines. Imagine for a moment that every single book search, user login, or purchase could be processed without causing other users to wait. The use of goroutines makes it possible to achieve this level of efficiency.

Sample Program: Concurrent Book Searches

Consider the situation where a user wants to search for books based on multiple genres simultaneously. Instead of querying the database sequentially for each genre, which would be time-consuming, we can leverage Goroutines.

```go
func searchBooksByGenre(genre string, ch chan<- []Book) {
    // Database search logic here
```

```
    books := dbSearch(genre)
    ch <- books
}

genres := []string{"Sci-Fi", "Fantasy", "Mystery"}
resultsChannel := make(chan []Book, len(genres))

for _, genre := range genres {
    go searchBooksByGenre(genre, resultsChannel)
}

var allBooks []Book
for i := 0; i < len(genres); i++ {
    books := <-resultsChannel
    allBooks = append(allBooks, books...)
}
```

In the above sample program, each genre search happens concurrently. Once all searches are complete, the results are aggregated.

Beyond searches, Goroutines excel in data-intensive operations. Suppose the GitforGits Bookstore wants to process user reviews to derive sentiments (positive, negative, neutral). Instead of processing each review one-by-one, it's efficient to process multiple reviews concurrently.

```
func processReview(review Review, ch chan<- Sentiment) {
    sentiment := deriveSentiment(review)
    ch <- sentiment
}

reviews := fetchPendingReviews()
sentimentsChannel := make(chan Sentiment, len(reviews))

for _, review := range reviews {
    go processReview(review, sentimentsChannel)
}
```

```go
var sentiments []Sentiment
for i := 0; i < len(reviews); i++ {
    sentiment := <-sentimentsChannel
    sentiments = append(sentiments, sentiment)
}
```

Although Goroutines have the potential to significantly improve performance, it is important to use them with caution. It's not a good idea to automatically generate a Goroutine for every insignificant task. It is of the utmost importance to identify situations in which concurrency brings tangible benefits, such as operations that are bound by input/output (I/O), tasks that are data-intensive, or computations that are CPU-intensive. Tasks such as batch processing of orders, parallel searches, and background tasks such as generating recommendations could fall under this category for the GitforGits Bookstore.

Goroutines Channeling

Need of Channels

While Goroutines grant GitforGits Bookstore the power of concurrent operations, they raise a pivotal question: how do these concurrently running Goroutines communicate safely? Enter Go's channels—a means of conveying data between Goroutines. Think of channels as pipes where data is sent from one end and received at the other. They are inherently synchronized, meaning they're designed to handle data safely without the pitfalls of race conditions.

Consider a scenario in which multiple Goroutines are responsible for updating a shared database in the GitforGits Bookstore's environment. It is possible that you will run into situations in which Goroutines will conflict with each other or overwrite each other's data if you do not have a mechanism like channels. Channels provide a synchronized means of exchanging data, which helps to ensure that data integrity is maintained. In essence, they bridge the gap, transforming isolated Goroutines into a community that is integrated and shares data.

Using Channels

Creating a channel is as straightforward as defining its type. If our bookstore needed a channel to pass book titles as strings, it'd be: bookChannel := make(chan string). To send data, you'd use the send statement: bookChannel <- "Golang in Action", and to receive data, you'd employ: title := <-bookChannel.

Sometimes, you'll want a Goroutine to only send or only receive data to ensure safety. Go supports this through channel directions. Consider our bookstore processing orders. An 'order processing' Goroutine might only send data, while a 'billing' Goroutine might only receive.

```
func processOrder(ch chan<- Order) {
    // Logic to process order
    ch <- newOrder
}

func billOrder(ch <-chan Order) {
    order := <-ch
    // Billing logic here
}
```

By specifying channel directions, you're setting clear boundaries, ensuring that Goroutines adhere to their designated roles.

Buffered Channels

By default, channels block—they pause the Goroutine until the receiver is ready (and vice versa). However, there might be scenarios in our bookstore where you'd like a bit of leeway—a buffer. Buffered channels let you specify a capacity. For example, bufferedChannel := make(chan int, 50) creates a channel for integers with a buffer for 50. With buffering, the sending Goroutine can continue even if the receiver isn't ready, provided the buffer isn't full.

Closing Channels

At times, you'll need to signify that no more data will be sent on a channel, essentially closing the communication line. This can be done using the close function. For our bookstore, after sending all available book titles, you might close the channel. Receivers can detect this closure, allowing them to stop waiting for new data. This is especially useful with the range keyword, iterating over values until the channel closes.

```
for title := range bookChannel {
    // Process each title
}
```

Multiplexing Channel Operations

Imagine if our bookstore needed to listen to multiple channels simultaneously—perhaps one for orders, another for feedback. The select statement enables just that, allowing a Goroutine to wait on multiple communication operations. Paired with the default clause, it can prevent the

Goroutine from blocking when no channels are ready.

```
select {
case order := <-ordersChannel:
    // Process order
case feedback := <-feedbackChannel:
    // Handle feedback
default:
    // None are ready; perhaps log an idle timestamp
}
```

By incorporating Goroutines and channels, our GitforGits Bookstore application moves beyond just concurrency, rather it attains a harmonized concurrent operation where data flows seamlessly, tasks synchronize effectively, and the system's integrity remains uncompromised.

Up and Running with Synchronization
Importance of Synchronization

Goroutines, by their very nature, introduce a level of complexity when multiple threads operate concurrently. This concurrency, while powerful, can lead to intricate challenges, particularly around managing shared resources and ensuring operations complete in a controlled manner. Without proper synchronization, concurrent operations can interfere with each other, leading to race conditions or data inconsistencies, which can significantly hamper the reliability and integrity of an application.

To mitigate such concurrency-related issues, Go provides robust synchronization tools, namely sync.WaitGroup and sync.Mutex. The sync.WaitGroup is essential for scenarios where there's a need to wait for a collection of Goroutines to finish executing. It allows the program to block until all goroutines have completed their tasks, ensuring a coordinated workflow. On the other hand, sync.Mutex (mutual exclusion) plays a crucial role in protecting shared resources. It ensures that only one Goroutine accesses a particular section of code at a time, preventing simultaneous access that could lead to data corruption or unexpected behavior.

sync.WaitGroup

Think about the following scenario: you start multiple Goroutines to retrieve book details, but before you can send a consolidated list to the user, you have to wait for all of them to finish what they are doing. To sync, enter.WaitGroup functions as a counter; you add one to it for each Goroutine that you initiate, and you subtract one from it when a Goroutine completes. When this occurs, the primary function is able to wait until the counter has returned to zero.

Let us say the bookstore wants to retrieve information about books from both categories at the same time.

```
var wg sync.WaitGroup

func fetchBooks(category string) {
    defer wg.Done()
    // Fetching logic here
}

categories := []string{"Thriller", "Sci-Fi", "History"}
for _, category := range categories {
    wg.Add(1)
    go fetchBooks(category)
}

wg.Wait() // This will block until all book fetches are complete
```

By utilizing WaitGroup, the main function holds off until all book details are gathered, ensuring the user gets a comprehensive list.

sync.Mutex

As the application grows, it's common to have multiple Goroutines executing concurrently, often needing to access and modify shared resources, such as the inventory database. Imagine a scenario where multiple Goroutines attempt to update the inventory count of a specific book simultaneously. Without a mechanism to manage this concurrency, these simultaneous operations could overlap, leading to data inconsistencies, such as incorrect inventory counts, and potentially causing significant issues in inventory management and customer experience. This is where sync.Mutex becomes an invaluable tool in the Go programmer's arsenal. Acting as a mutual exclusion lock, sync.Mutex ensures that only one Goroutine can access or modify a shared resource at any given time. When a Goroutine accesses a section of code protected by a Mutex, it locks the Mutex, performs its operations, and then unlocks the Mutex upon completion.

For instance, when updating the book inventory in GitforGits Bookstore, wrapping the update logic with sync.Mutex ensures that when one Goroutine is updating the inventory count, no other Goroutine can modify it until the operation is complete. This protection mechanism is critical in preventing scenarios like double decrementing of a book count, which could occur if two Goroutines try to reduce the inventory simultaneously without understanding that another

Goroutine is already making a similar change.

Consider the task of updating book inventory after a sale.

```go
var mutex sync.Mutex
var inventory = make(map[string]int)

func updateInventory(bookName string, sold int) {
    mutex.Lock() // Locking the critical section
    inventory[bookName] -= sold
    mutex.Unlock() // Releasing the lock
}
```

With Mutex guarding the inventory update, even if multiple Goroutines execute this function, each update will be sequential, preserving data integrity.

Combining WaitGroup and Mutex

During your experience of using the bookstore app, there may be situations in which you are required to wait for multiple Goroutines to complete their tasks while simultaneously ensuring that the shared resources that are accessed by these Goroutines are safeguarded. There is potential for a high level of efficiency when WaitGroup is used for orchestration and Mutex is used for resource protection.

Imagine if our bookstore had to process bulk orders, each potentially updating multiple book inventories.

```go
var wg sync.WaitGroup
var mutex sync.Mutex

func processOrder(order Order) {
    defer wg.Done()

    for _, item := range order.Items {
        mutex.Lock() // Ensure only one Goroutine updates the inventory
        inventory[item.BookName] -= item.Quantity
        mutex.Unlock()
```

```
    }
}

bulkOrders := fetchBulkOrders()
for _, order := range bulkOrders {
    wg.Add(1)
    go processOrder(order)
}

wg.Wait()
```

Both these tools ensure that the application reaps the benefits of concurrent processing, and while it does so, it also should never compromise on data consistency, user experience, or system stability.

Implement Concurrent Cache

Fetching details of a popular book repeatedly from a database can be resource-intensive and slow. A cache stores these frequent data retrievals in memory, offering speedier access. But, when we introduce concurrent operations, managing this cache without data clashes becomes crucial. This is where the concurrent cache enters the scene, ensuring fast data access while maintaining data integrity in the face of simultaneous access.

The concurrent cache will be a map to store book details and a sync.Mutex to ensure concurrent safety. This structure safeguards our cache from concurrent writes, which could compromise its integrity.

```
type ConcurrentCache struct {
    data  map[string]*BookDetails
    mutex sync.Mutex
}
```

When a book detail is fetched, it's stored in the cache for future quick access. Following is how you'd safely add data to our cache:

```
func (c *ConcurrentCache) Store(key string, value *BookDetails) {
    c.mutex.Lock() // Locking for concurrent safety
```

```
    c.data[key] = value
    c.mutex.Unlock() // Always remember to unlock
}
```

Retrieving data is equally straightforward. However, we don't need to lock the cache for read operations as map reads are safe in concurrent scenarios. Still, for complete isolation from any writes that might be happening, we can use the mutex.

```
func (c *ConcurrentCache) Fetch(key string) (*BookDetails, bool) {
    c.mutex.Lock()
    value, exists := c.data[key]
    c.mutex.Unlock()
    return value, exists
}
```

A cache without eviction might grow indefinitely. In our bookstore, if an item is less accessed or if the cache gets too large, we should remove some entries. A simple Least Recently Used (LRU) strategy can be employed. This would involve tracking access times and removing the least accessed items. But, for brevity, we shall consider a simple size-based eviction.

```
const MAX_CACHE_SIZE = 1000 // for instance

func (c *ConcurrentCache) CheckEviction() {
    c.mutex.Lock()
    if len(c.data) > MAX_CACHE_SIZE {
        for key := range c.data {
            delete(c.data, key) // Simplified eviction
            break
        }
    }
    c.mutex.Unlock()
}
```

Let us say a user is interested in purchasing a book. First, the application examines the cache. In the event that the book details are stored in the cache, they are returned without delay. If this is not the case, the application will retrieve the information from the database, save it in the cache for use in response to subsequent requests, and then send it back to the user. Because of this configuration, popular books, which are books that are accessed frequently, will soon be stored in the cache, which will result in faster response times.

Parallelism vs. Concurrency

Unveiling Parallelism

The need to do more with less time is fundamental to contemporary computational systems. Taking advantage of the multi-core architectures found in modern CPUs, parallelism allows for the simultaneous execution of multiple tasks or processes. Each lane on a multi-lane highway stands in for a core, and the cars zipping along them stand in for processes running in parallel. In contrast, on a single-lane road, vehicles will have to wait in line and, no matter how fast they go, will not be able to match the throughput of a multi-lane highway.

Contrarily to parallelism, which emphasizes doing many things simultaneously, concurrency emphasizes managing many things simultaneously. Simultaneous execution is not always implied by concurrency. Rather, it is concerned with the non-blocking coordination of individual jobs. To continue with our road analogy, concurrency would be like a single lane of traffic where vehicles are continuously entering and exiting, moving forward and stopping at signals, but constantly checking to make sure there are no delays.

Think about two possible situations. One is that the store experiences an influx of thousands of users during a flash sale. Not all of these requests need to be processed at once, but the system should handle them all so no user has to wait too long. In this context, concurrency really excels. A seamless user experience is guaranteed by the efficient management of each request, which is a Goroutine.

Now the second situation is that the bookshop decides to make book recommendations after looking at each customer's 100 most recent purchases. If done sequentially, analyzing these purchases for thousands of users would take a lot of time. But if the system splits the work among numerous CPU cores and runs them all at once, the job finishes a lot quicker. Right here we see parallelism at work.

Sample Program: Book Recommendation Function

To illustrate, we shall consider a book recommendation function:

```
func analyzePurchases(user User) []BookRecommendations {
    // Code to analyze user's purchases and return recommendations
}
```

Using concurrency (with Goroutines) for managing many user requests:

```go
users := fetchUsers()
for _, user := range users {
    go analyzePurchases(user) // Goroutines handle multiple users concurrently
}
```

But, for true parallelism, one might use Go's parallelism feature in testing:

```go
import "testing"

func BenchmarkRecommendations(b *testing.B) {
    users := fetchSampleUsersForBenchmarking()
    b.RunParallel(func(pb *testing.PB) {
        for pb.Next() {
            for _, user := range users {
                analyzePurchases(user) // Run in parallel across multiple cores
            }
        }
    })
}
```

While both parallelism and concurrency aim to optimize the system's performance, their approach and use-cases can differ.

Do's and Don'ts
Do Understand Concurrency vs Parallelism
Start by understanding the distinction between concurrency and parallelism. While they are often used interchangeably, they address different aspects of computation. As we previously learned, concurrency is about managing multiple tasks at once—it doesn't necessarily mean things happen at the same time. Parallelism, however, is about doing multiple things at the same time, leveraging multiple CPU cores. In the context of GitforGits, concurrency will primarily help handle user requests efficiently. While parallelism can speed up heavy computational tasks, the bookstore's primary challenge is handling numerous user interactions, making concurrency the tool of choice.

Don't Neglect Data Races

A common pitfall in concurrent programming is the data race, where two goroutines access the same variable concurrently, and at least one of the accesses is a write. This can lead to unpredictable results and hard-to-diagnose bugs. When multiple parts of your application, say different goroutines, try to read and write to shared resources, ensure synchronization mechanisms like sync.Mutex are in place to prevent simultaneous access.

Do Use Goroutines Sparingly

Goroutines are lightweight and efficient, but that doesn't mean they should be spawned recklessly. Every goroutine consumes resources. If GitforGits were to start a new goroutine for every minor task, it could lead to resource exhaustion. It's essential to strike a balance. Use goroutines for tasks that genuinely benefit from concurrent execution, like handling independent user requests or performing non-blocking operations.

Don't Forget to Handle Goroutine Panics

In Go, a panic is a runtime error. If unhandled, a panic in a goroutine can bring down the entire application. Implementing defer-recover mechanisms can help catch and handle panics, ensuring that even if one goroutine encounters an issue, the entire application remains stable. In the bookstore context, if a goroutine handling a user request encounters a problem, it shouldn't affect other users' experiences.

Do Limit the Number of Goroutines

While goroutines are lightweight, there's still overhead. Spawning thousands or millions without control could lead to performance issues or even crash the system. Using tools like buffered channels or worker pools can help control the number of concurrently executing goroutines. For GitforGits, this might mean limiting the number of simultaneous book searches or user logins, ensuring the system remains responsive even under heavy load.

Don't Ignore Proper Shutdown Procedures

When the application needs to shut down, perhaps for an update or due to some issue, it should do so gracefully. This means ensuring all running goroutines have completed their tasks. By implementing a graceful shutdown procedure, you ensure that no user requests are abruptly terminated, providing a smooth user experience.

Do Always Test Concurrency

It's easy to introduce errors when dealing with concurrency. Therefore, always test concurrent parts of the application rigorously. Using Go's in-built testing tools can help simulate different scenarios and ensure the system behaves as expected. For GitforGits, this could involve simulating numerous simultaneous book purchases or user registrations, ensuring the system can handle the load without errors.

Concurrency, when used judiciously, can significantly enhance the performance of GitforGits Bookstore. However, with its power comes responsibility. Adhering to these do's and don'ts can ensure that the system is both efficient and robust, offering users a seamless and speedy experience.

Summary

In this chapter, we have focused on how to make the most of concurrency, with a specific focus on the GitforGits Bookstore. The ability to efficiently handle numerous tasks, regardless of their timing, is known as concurrency. This means handling various user interactions, such as perusing books and making purchases, and making sure they all work smoothly no matter how many users are using it at the same time.

Knowing how concurrency differs from parallelism has been crucial. There is a difference between the two, despite the fact that they both seek to maximize efficiency. Concurrency is great for handling a variety of user requests because it is great at handling multiple tasks at once. The major emphasis here is not on parallelism, but taking advantage of multi-core CPU architectures to run numerous tasks simultaneously is. To guarantee that user interactions are timely and seamless, GitforGits places a premium on concurrency.

There was a lot of learning about how to put concurrency into practice, specifically about using goroutines. Be careful when using gouroutines, even though they are lightweight. Overconsumption can cause resources to be exhausted. Data races happen when numerous processes try to access the same shared resource at the same time; to prevent them, it is crucial to use suitable synchronization techniques like sync.Mutex. When runtime errors happen inside goroutines, there must be error-handling mechanisms like defer-recovery to handle them. The entire application will not be compromised in the event that one routine fails. Additionally, it was emphasized that thorough concurrency testing, allowing active goroutines to finish their tasks, and performing proper system shutdowns are essential practices.

Request management is a top priority for the GitforGits Bookstore. In order to accomplish this, this chapter outlined the various approaches and methods that could be employed in conjunction with concurrency. In order to keep the system running smoothly for the bookshop, it has been necessary to learn both the basics and dive into more complex subjects like goroutines, synchronization, error handling, and testing.

Chapter 7: Sessions, Authentication, and Authorization

User Sessions Overview

User experience is of the utmost importance in web applications, and it frequently determines whether a platform is successful or unsuccessful. The application of the concept of sessions is essential to the delivery of a streamlined and individualized user experience. Sessions are not only essential for ensuring that user interactions remain consistent, but they also represent a temporary and interactive exchange of information between the user and the application under consideration. When it comes to web applications such as the GitforGits Bookstore, sessions are the most important factor in ensuring that users have a consistent experience regardless of whether they are navigating through different pages or returning after a break.

Think about a user who is looking through the GitforGits Bookstore. During the time that they are browsing, searching for books, adding items to their shopping cart, and reading reviews, sessions play an important part in maintaining the continuity of this interaction. In the absence of sessions, the navigation of each page would result in a loss of context, which would make the user's experience more disjointed and frustrating. Sessions are an effective means of bridging this gap. In the context of GitforGits, sessions make it possible to store essential user data, such as the contents of a user's shopping cart, their search history, and any personalized settings or recommendations they may have made. This helps to ensure that the user's shopping experience is smooth and uninterrupted.

Sessions are useful for more than just ensuring continuity; they also play an important role in the process of personalizing the user experience. Internet users in the modern era have come to anticipate a personalized experience whenever they visit online platforms. There are many different ways that personalization can be implemented in a bookstore setting, including making book recommendations based on previous purchases and viewing history, as well as sending out personal greetings. During sessions, the GitforGits Bookstore is able to store and retrieve data that is specific to each individual customer. This makes it possible for each customer to have a shopping experience that is both personalized and interesting.

The significance of sessions, on the other hand, is not restricted to the user experience alone; they are also extremely important for the purposes of security. Consider, for example, the system of user authentication. It is both impractical and insecure for users to have to re-enter their credentials each time they access a new page on the GitforGits platform after they have already had the opportunity to log in. Sessions are able to address this issue by preserving the authenticated state of the user, which enables seamless navigation under their profile after they have successfully logged in. Because of this convenience, secure session management is extremely important, as any breach in security could result in vulnerabilities such as unauthorized access or data breaches.

For GitforGits, the management of an increasing number of concurrent sessions presents a formidable challenge as the user base continues to grow through its expansion. When it comes to session management, the scalability and efficiency of the system become extremely important factors. To accomplish this, it is necessary to make strategic decisions regarding the storage of session data, whether it be in-memory, databases, or distributed systems, and to devise methods for ensuring that data access is both quick and free of bottlenecks. The objective is to make certain that the performance and dependability of session handling mechanisms do not suffer as a result of an increase in the number of users, but rather scale proportionately to meet the growing demand. For our Bookstore, mastering this aspect is not merely an enhancement; rather, it is a necessity. This is because it guarantees that users will have a safe, personalized, and uninterrupted browsing experience, regardless of the growth and scale of the platform.

Store Session Data
Session Storage Options
Multiple options are available to choose from when it comes to the storage of session data. Generally speaking, session data can be stored on the client-side, the server-side, or in external storage systems such as databases or caching systems. Every single approach comes with its own set of benefits and difficulties.

Client-Side Session Storage
Client-side storage involves keeping session data on the user's device, typically within cookies. This method is straightforward and doesn't require any server-side storage resources. However, it poses some challenges:
- Limited Storage: Browsers restrict the amount of data that can be stored in cookies. This limitation can be problematic for the GitforGits Bookstore if there's a need to store large session data.
- Security Concerns: Client-side storage can be vulnerable to attacks. Therefore, sensitive data should never be stored on the client side without proper encryption.

For example, you can set a cookie with session data like this:

```
http.SetCookie(w, &http.Cookie{
    Name:    "session_token",
    Value:   "some_token_value",
    Expires: time.Now().Add(72 * time.Hour),
})
```

Server-Side Session Storage
Storing session data on the server offers more flexibility and security. The client is typically given a unique session ID, which is then used to fetch the session data from the server. This method is

scalable and can handle larger data sets.
- Memory-Based Storage: One can store session data directly in the application's memory. However, it's volatile; if the application restarts, the data is lost.
- File-Based Storage: This involves writing session data to files on the server. It's more persistent than memory storage but can become slow with a large number of concurrent sessions.

For example, using File-Based Storage:

```
// Using gorilla/sessions package
store := sessions.NewFilesystemStore("", []byte("secret-key"))
session, _ := store.Get(r, "session-name")
session.Values["user_id"] = "12345"
session.Save(r, w)
```

External Session Storage

Larger web apps prefer external storage solutions for scalability and reliability. Databases (like PostgreSQL or MySQL) or caching systems (like Redis) are popular choices.

For example using Redis:

```
// Using redistore
store, err := redistore.NewRediStore(10, "tcp", ":6379", "", []byte("secret-key"))
session, _ := store.Get(r, "session-name")
session.Values["user_id"] = "12345"
session.Save(r, w)
```

Security and Session Storage

Regardless of the storage option chosen, security must be paramount. Always ensure session data, especially sensitive information, is encrypted. Use HTTPS to prevent session hijacking or man-in-the-middle attacks.

Given the potential scale and need for reliable session management, using a caching system like Redis for fast access, backed by a database for persistence, would provide both performance and reliability. Depending on the specific requirements and scale of the application, the optimal solution might differ.

Secure Cookie Handling

Secure Cookies Overview

Web applications rely heavily on cookies for session tracking, state maintenance, and user preference storage. The security of cookies, on the other hand, has become of the utmost importance in light of the numerous cyber threats that are looming in the digital world. The implementation of secure cookie handling practices is a non-negotiable requirement, particularly in applications such as the GitforGits Bookstore, which involve user data and possibly transactional information.

Cookies, when mishandled, can become gateways for malicious attackers. Two of the major threats include:
- Cross-Site Scripting (XSS): An attacker injects malicious scripts into web pages viewed by users. If the script runs and accesses the cookie, it can send this data to the attacker.
- Cross-Site Request Forgery (CSRF): An attacker tricks a victim into performing actions they didn't intend to. If the victim is authenticated, the attacker can make requests on their behalf using their session cookie.

Implementing HTTPOnly Attribute

Secure cookie handling is a cornerstone of web application security, especially when dealing with sensitive user data. Implementing the HTTPOnly attribute is one of the initial yet crucial steps in this direction. By setting this attribute, cookies become inaccessible to JavaScript running in the browser. This simple measure can significantly bolster your application's defenses against Cross-Site Scripting (XSS) attacks. Even in the event of an XSS breach, the attacker would be unable to exploit the cookies, as JavaScript cannot manipulate them.

```
http.SetCookie(w, &http.Cookie{
    Name:     "session_token",
    Value:    "some_token_value",
    HTTPOnly: true,
})
```

Secure Cookies with Secure Attribute

Another critical aspect is the implementation of the Secure attribute in cookies. This attribute ensures that cookies are transmitted only over secure, encrypted HTTPS connections. Its importance becomes particularly pronounced in scenarios involving user authentication or the transmission of sensitive information. By enforcing this attribute, you assure that cookies are not inadvertently sent over unsecured HTTP connections, which are prone to eavesdropping or man-in-the-middle attacks.

```
http.SetCookie(w, &http.Cookie{
    Name:   "session_token",
    Value:  "some_token_value",
    Secure: true,
})
```

SameSite Attribute

The SameSite attribute is another powerful tool in the cookie security arsenal. It offers a layer of protection against Cross-Site Request Forgery (CSRF) attacks. By setting this attribute to Strict, you ensure that cookies are sent only when the request originates from the same site, thereby significantly reducing the risk of CSRF attacks where cookies might be sent along with requests initiated from third-party sites.

```
http.SetCookie(w, &http.Cookie{
    Name:     "session_token",
    Value:    "some_token_value",
    SameSite: http.SameSiteStrictMode,
})
```

Encrypting Cookie Values

Beyond these attributes, encrypting the values stored in cookies adds an extra layer of security. In the unfortunate event of cookie interception, encryption ensures that the contents remain a riddle to the interceptor. Go's standard library offers robust packages, such as crypto/aes, which can be utilized for effective encryption and decryption. This encryption is particularly crucial for cookies carrying sensitive information like session tokens or personal identifiers.

Moreover, setting an expiration time for cookies is a vital practice. By defining a specific duration for the cookie's validity, you minimize the risk window. Cookies that linger indefinitely pose a greater security risk, as they offer a prolonged opportunity for exploitation. Setting a reasonable expiration period, such as the duration of a user session or a predefined time limit, can significantly mitigate this risk.

```
http.SetCookie(w, &http.Cookie{
    Name:    "session_token",
    Value:   "some_token_value",
    Expires: time.Now().Add(2 * time.Hour),
```

})

In conclusion, as Bruce Schneier aptly puts it, "Security is not a product, but a process." This mantra holds especially true in the context of web application security. The implementation of robust cookie handling mechanisms, such as HTTPOnly, Secure, and SameSite attributes, alongside encryption and prudent expiration settings, forms a critical part of this ongoing process. As an author, I emphasize the importance of vigilance, prioritizing security in design decisions, and staying abreast with the latest security practices and vulnerabilities. Continuously evolving and fortifying the security measures will ensure a fortified defense for your web application against emerging threats.

Implement User Authentication

Every web application that stores user-specific data or functionalities is required to have an authentication mechanism in place. Through the use of user authentication, GitforGits Bookstore is able to provide customers with a personalized shopping experience, as well as maintain user profiles and keep track of previous purchases. In addition to improving the user experience, it also strengthens the security of our application by ensuring that only authorized users are able to access particular functionalities or data.

Setting up Database

Our bookstore application must store user credentials in a database. However, for security reasons, it's not advisable to store plain-text passwords. Instead, we will store a hashed version. When a user tries to log in, the system hashes the entered password and compares it with the stored hash.

```go
type User struct {
    ID       int
    Username string
    Password string // This will store the hashed password
}
```

Registering New User

When a new user signs up, their entered password should be hashed before storage. Go offers the bcrypt library for this purpose, which is renowned for its security robustness.

```go
import "golang.org/x/crypto/bcrypt"
```

```go
func RegisterUser(username, password string) error {
    hashedPassword, err := bcrypt.GenerateFromPassword([]byte(password), bcrypt.DefaultCost)
    if err != nil {
        return err
    }

    // Store the user with the hashed password in the database.
}
```

Logging In an Existing User

During login, the user provides their credentials. The system then retrieves the hashed password associated with the entered username from the database, hashes the provided password, and compares the two. If they match, the user is authenticated.

```go
func LoginUser(username, enteredPassword string) bool {
    // Retrieve the hashed password from the database based on the username
    storedHashedPassword := // retrieve from database

    err := bcrypt.CompareHashAndPassword(storedHashedPassword, []byte(enteredPassword))
    if err != nil {
        return false // authentication failed
    }
    return true // authentication successful
}
```

Managing User Sessions

Once the user is authenticated, the application needs to maintain that state so that the user doesn't have to re-authenticate with every request. This is achieved using sessions. After successful authentication, a session token is generated and sent to the user as a cookie. This token is then used to verify the user's identity on subsequent requests.

Logging Out User

Logging out essentially means invalidating the user's session. To accomplish this, the session token is deleted from both the server and the client-side.

```
func LogoutUser(sessionToken string) {
    // Remove the session token from server storage
    // Send a response to the client to delete the session cookie
}
```

Protect and Secure User Passwords

In the early days of the World Wide Web, it was not unusual for applications to store user passwords in databases in plain text format. An extremely high level of security risk is posed by this approach, which is analogous to leaving the doors of user accounts wide open. Within the context of an application such as the GitforGits Bookstore, the protection of user passwords is just as important as the protection of the books themselves. It is possible that any breach that exposes plain-text passwords could have severe consequences, putting the trust of users and the integrity of applications at risk.

Hashing

Hashing plays a crucial role in password security. It involves transforming a password into a fixed-size sequence of bytes, usually a lengthy string of numbers and letters. This process is one-way; while you can generate a hash from the original password, it's computationally infeasible to revert a hash back to its original form. Thus, when a user logs in, the application hashes the entered password and compares this hash against the one stored in the database. If they match, the user is granted access.

Given below is a simple example using Go's bcrypt package:

```
import "golang.org/x/crypto/bcrypt"

hashedPassword, err := bcrypt.GenerateFromPassword([]byte(plainPassword), bcrypt.DefaultCost)
```

Salting

However, hashing alone has vulnerabilities. Attackers can use precomputed tables (rainbow tables) to crack hashes. Salting addresses this issue. It involves adding a unique random sequence of characters (salt) to each password before hashing. Consequently, even identical passwords will produce different hashes.

```go
func hashPasswordWithSalt(plainPassword, salt string) (string, error) {
    combinedPassword := salt + plainPassword
    hashedPassword, err := bcrypt.GenerateFromPassword([]byte(combinedPassword), bcrypt.DefaultCost)
    return string(hashedPassword), err
}
```

Pepper

While a salt is stored with the hash, a pepper adds another layer of security. It's a secret value mixed into every password before hashing, stored separately from the database, potentially offline. Thus, even if an attacker gains database access, without the pepper, they can't accurately recreate hashes.

Implementing a pepper involves adding it to the password-salting process:

```go
const pepper = "your-secret-pepper"

func hashPasswordWithSaltAndPepper(plainPassword, salt string) (string, error) {
    combinedPassword := salt + plainPassword + pepper
    hashedPassword, err := bcrypt.GenerateFromPassword([]byte(combinedPassword), bcrypt.DefaultCost)
    return string(hashedPassword), err
}
```

Iterations

Brute force attacks involve trying every possible combination until the right password is found. To render these attacks impractical, we use iterative hashing. By hashing the password thousands, or even millions of times, we significantly slow down the verification process. This minimal delay is imperceptible to users but makes brute-forcing infeasible for attackers.

Up-to-date Algorithms

Cryptographic methods evolve. What's considered secure today might be vulnerable tomorrow. It's crucial to stay updated with current cryptographic standards and be ready to migrate to stronger algorithms. Libraries like bcrypt automatically handle many complexities, but developers must be vigilant and proactive.

Beyond these methods, follow general security guidelines. Use HTTPS to ensure passwords aren't intercepted during transmission. Implement security headers to protect against attacks like Cross-site Scripting (XSS), which could be used to steal passwords. Regularly audit your code and dependencies for vulnerabilities.

Implement and Operate OAuth

'Login with Google' or 'Login with Facebook' buttons are examples of buttons that are frequently found in contemporary web applications and so it does in GitforGits Bookstore. OAuth is a standardized protocol that enables third-party applications to access user data without revealing the user's password. These buttons are the defining characteristics of OAuth. The integration of OAuth into GitforGits Bookstore would make it possible for users to quickly gain access to the platform without having to create a new account, which would significantly improve the user experience.

Understanding OAuth

OAuth (Open Authorization) is a token-based authentication process. Instead of sharing passwords, applications request tokens from a central server and use these tokens to prove identity. This process involves redirecting a user to the OAuth provider, where they log in, and then return with an access token. GitforGits can then use this token to fetch required data, like the user's name or email, from the provider.

The choice of an OAuth provider is paramount. For our bookstore, we might consider popular providers like Google, Facebook, or Twitter. Each comes with its own set of APIs, user base, and considerations. For instance, while Google offers a vast user base, Facebook might offer richer demographic data.

Setting up OAuth

To begin integrating OAuth, register the GitforGits app with the desired provider. This registration provides crucial credentials like the client ID and client secret.

```
import (
        "golang.org/x/oauth2"
        "golang.org/x/oauth2/google"
)

conf := &oauth2.Config{
        ClientID:     "YOUR_CLIENT_ID",
        ClientSecret: "YOUR_CLIENT_SECRET",
```

```
        RedirectURL: "https://gitforgits.com/oauth/callback",
        Scopes:      []string{"profile", "email"},
        Endpoint:     google.Endpoint,
}
```

This configuration initializes OAuth with the chosen provider, in this case, Google.

Redirection and Callbacks

After setup, direct users to the OAuth provider's authentication page. Post authentication, the provider redirects users back to the GitforGits app, specifically to the provided RedirectURL, carrying with them an authorization code.

```
http.HandleFunc("/login", func(w http.ResponseWriter, r *http.Request) {
        url := conf.AuthCodeURL("state", oauth2.AccessTypeOffline)
        http.Redirect(w, r, url, http.StatusFound)
})


http.HandleFunc("/oauth/callback", func(w http.ResponseWriter, r *http.Request) {
        code := r.URL.Query().Get("code")
        token, err := conf.Exchange(oauth2.NoContext, code)
        // Handle the token and create or authenticate the user in the bookstore app.
})
```

Once you have the token, use it to fetch user details. With Google, for instance, you might retrieve the user's Google profile, extracting their name, profile picture, and email.

Also, OAuth tokens are short-lived, so they often come with a refresh token. Use this refresh token to get a new access token without redirecting the user to the OAuth provider again. Also, always use HTTPS for OAuth transactions to ensure data integrity and confidentiality.

Summary

This chapter delves into the complex subject of sessions, emphasizing their significance in maintaining continuity and customizing user experiences in GitforGits Bookstore. Sessions are essential for distinguishing and recalling users across multiple requests, allowing for customized interactions. The chapter not only laid the groundwork for sessions, but also delves into the complexities of storing session data, ensuring that developers are adequately prepared to handle user data in a secure and efficient manner.

Our journey then took us into the subject of cookies, which are tiny data fragments stored on users' web browsers. We learned how to manage cookies effectively, particularly in relation to sessions, in order to ensure the security and protection of user data. This understanding was especially important when we switched to user authentication. The chapter provided a detailed manual for implementing a secure login/logout system, ensuring that users can securely access their accounts and have confidence in the GitforGits Bookstore's data protection measures. The primary emphasis was on the implementation of password storage methods, with a special emphasis on the importance of encryption. This serves as a safeguard against potential security breaches and unauthorized entry.

The chapter advanced our understanding by incorporating OAuth, a widely used method for third-party authentication. OAuth allows users to authenticate and access applications using their existing accounts, such as Google or Facebook, avoiding the need to create new login credentials. This not only improves user experience but also security by lowering the risk associated with password management. With the help of practical illustrations and code excerpts, we were guided through the entire OAuth cycle, from selecting a provider to retrieving user information using tokens. Finally, the chapter concluded with an in-depth exploration of advanced concepts, such as refreshing tokens, to ensure the GitforGits Bookstore's ongoing efficiency and user-friendliness, even as sessions evolve and change.

Chapter 8: Frontend and Backend Communication

Frontend-Backend Overview

Web applications have transformed our interaction with the internet by delivering dynamic and personalized user experiences. This transformation is dependent on the seamless integration of these applications' frontend and backend. The backend, also known as the "server-side," is the functional heart of an application. It is in charge of the application's business logic, data storage, and critical operations. In contrast, the frontend or "client-side" is what users interact with directly. It includes all visible to users elements such as text, images, graphics, and animations and is critical in shaping the overall user experience.

The backend of our GitforGits Bookstore project handles critical tasks like verifying user credentials, retrieving book lists, and processing purchases. It enables direct database interactions, validates data, and executes the core logic of various operations. The efficiency of the backend, enabled by frameworks such as Go's net/http package, ensures quick database interactions, security, and scalability as the user base grows. Without a solid backend, the application may encounter issues such as data loss or delayed user request processing.

Meanwhile, the frontend visualizes these backend processes for the user. When a user enters the GitforGits Bookstore, they interact with graphical elements such as forms and dashboards rather than the underlying database queries or server-side computations. These frontend interactions are governed by technologies such as HTML, CSS, and JavaScript. A well-designed frontend ensures seamless navigation and optimal rendering across multiple devices, which has a direct impact on the user's interaction quality and overall experience.

The true essence of a web application's functionality, on the other hand, lies in the effective communication between its frontend and backend. When a user searches for a book on GitforGits, for example, the frontend captures and forwards the request to the backend. The backend then retrieves the necessary information and relays it to the frontend, which displays the results to the user. APIs (Application Programming Interfaces) facilitate this interaction, forming the critical link that enables the dynamic web experiences that users enjoy.

Furthermore, the introduction of modern JavaScript frameworks and single-page applications (SPAs) such as React or Vue.js has blurred the traditional frontend-backend divide. By communicating with the backend via APIs, these SPAs can perform certain operations on the client side that were previously handled by the backend. This method improves the app's responsiveness and speed, resulting in a more seamless user experience.

Finally, the interaction between the frontend and backend is critical in modern web applications. Although they serve distinct purposes, their collaboration is what determines the efficacy and appeal of web platforms. Web applications like GitforGits Bookstore can provide both functional efficiency and a compelling user experience by ensuring both areas are well-designed and harmoniously integrated.

RESTful API Overview

The interoperability between systems, be it between different software applications or between frontend and backend components of the same application, is often enabled through Application Programming Interfaces (APIs). Among the various architectural styles of APIs, RESTful API, or simply REST, stands out as one of the most widely accepted practices. Embracing a set of constraints and principles, RESTful APIs are designed to tap into standard HTTP methods, making them simple to understand and use.

Background

Representational State Transfer (REST) was conceptualized by Roy Fielding in 2000. In essence, REST is an architectural style that employs standard HTTP methods, grounded in the principles of simplicity, scalability, and performance. A RESTful API is merely an API that adheres to the principles of REST. Drawing an analogy from our GitforGits Bookstore web application, consider the process of fetching details of a book. With RESTful services, this task involves a straightforward HTTP GET request, which returns the book details in a format like JSON or XML.

Stateless Interactions

A defining feature of REST is its statelessness. Every request from the client to the server must contain all the information needed to understand and process the request. To put it differently, the server should not retain any client state between requests. For instance, in GitforGits Bookstore, when a user wants to check out a book, they send a request to the server. The server processes it, sends back the relevant data, and does not remember anything about the user's state after the transaction. This approach ensures that each request can be processed independently, bolstering scalability and reliability.

Client-Server Architecture

REST is built upon the principle of separating the user interface concerns from the data storage concerns, making it a perfect fit for web applications. In GitforGits Bookstore, the frontend (client) interacts with the user, while the backend (server) manages the data. This separation allows both sides to evolve independently. The client only worries about rendering the data, while the server processes requests and manages data, ensuring a clear distribution of roles.

Uniform Interface

To simplify interactions and enhance visibility, REST mandates a uniform, consistent interface. This constraint dictates that the method of interaction with a RESTful API remains consistent, regardless of the type of application or platform consuming the API. For example, whether it's a mobile app or a web browser accessing GitforGits Bookstore, the method of requesting book details would be the same.

Layered System

RESTful APIs are designed to be layered. Each layer has a specific function, and each layer cannot "see" beyond the immediate layer with which it interacts. This modular design, such as separating the database layer from the business logic layer, fosters scalability and maintainability. In the context of GitforGits, it ensures that as the platform grows, components can be optimized or replaced independently without affecting others.

State Representations

When a client interacts with a server through a RESTful API, it communicates through representations, typically in the form of JSON or XML. This representation contains enough information for the client to modify or delete the resource on the server if needed. In the GitforGits Bookstore scenario, when fetching a book's details, the server might return a JSON representation of that book, encompassing title, author, price, and more.

For GitforGits Bookstore, these principles ensure that data flows efficiently, interfaces remain consistent, and the system as a whole remains robust and scalable.

Build My First API

An essential step in the process of establishing communication between the frontend and the backend is the preparation of an application programming interface (API) endpoint that will retrieve book information from our GitforGits Bookstore app. The procedure will be broken down into its component parts.

Project Initialization and Import Packages

Start with the initialization of the project and importing necessary packages. The net/http package from the Go standard library will be the primary package we'll use to set up our server and endpoints.

```go
package main

import (
        "net/http"
        "encoding/json"
)
```

Defining Book Structure

The next step is to define the data structure for a book. This will give clarity on what information a book holds.

```go
type Book struct {
    ID     int     `json:"id"`
    Title  string  `json:"title"`
    Author string  `json:"author"`
    Price  float64 `json:"price"`
}
```

Sample Data
For the sake of this example, we shall consider we have some sample data of books stored in a slice.

```go
var books = []Book{
    {ID: 1, Title: "Go Basics", Author: "John Doe", Price: 10.99},
    {ID: 2, Title: "Advanced Go", Author: "Jane Smith", Price: 15.49},
}
```

Creating Endpoint Function
Now, we shall create a function fetchBookDetails that will handle the HTTP request to fetch the details of a specific book.

```go
func fetchBookDetails(w http.ResponseWriter, r *http.Request) {
    // Fetch book ID from the URL parameter
    bookID := r.URL.Query().Get("id")
    for _, book := range books {
        if strconv.Itoa(book.ID) == bookID {
            // Convert the "book" variable to JSON
            json.NewEncoder(w).Encode(book)
            return
        }
    }
    // If book not found, return an error response
    w.WriteHeader(http.StatusNotFound)
```

```
        json.NewEncoder(w).Encode("Book not found")
}
```

Setting up Server
Now that the function to fetch book details is ready, let us set up the server to listen for requests.

```
func main() {
        http.HandleFunc("/book", fetchBookDetails)
        http.ListenAndServe(":8080", nil)
}
```

Testing Endpoint
With everything in place, run your Go application. Using a tool like Postman or simply a browser, navigate to http://localhost:8080/book?id=1 to fetch the details for the book with ID 1. The returned data should be in JSON format.

Although the above setup works, for a real-world application, you'd use additional packages and middleware to handle routes better, manage CORS, logging, etc. Additionally, you would move away from a static data slice and integrate with a persistent database. Also ensure your endpoints have proper error handling. For instance, if a user doesn't provide an 'id' or provides an invalid one, return a meaningful error message.

JSON and Its Importance
JSON, an acronym for JavaScript Object Notation, is a universally acknowledged data interchange format renowned for its lightweight and human-readable properties. Its ease of use for both humans and machines – simple to read and write for the former, and equally straightforward to parse and generate for the latter – marks it as a premier choice in web development. Initially rooted in JavaScript, JSON has transcended its origins to become a language-independent format, garnering widespread support across various programming languages, including Go, which is especially relevant in the context of our learning around the GitforGits Bookstore application.

The fundamental role of JSON in web development cannot be overstated. It serves as the backbone for data transmission between a server and a web application, as well as among web applications themselves. This pivotal role stems from its concise yet flexible syntax, which not only facilitates ease of data interchange but also ensures that the data is easily understood and manipulated by developers. For web applications built on JavaScript or that interact with JavaScript-heavy frontends, JSON's inherent compatibility with JavaScript is invaluable. It allows for seamless parsing and manipulation of JSON data within these applications, creating a fluid and efficient bridge between the server and the client side.

Basic JSON Structure

A JSON value can be an object, array, string, number, or one of the literals: true, false, or null. Objects are wrapped in curly braces {} and are an unordered collection of key-value pairs. Arrays are ordered lists of values, wrapped in square brackets []. Strings in JSON must be enclosed in double quotes.

Go offers native support for JSON encoding and decoding through its encoding/json package. To represent JSON data in Go, you typically use structs, but you can also use maps.

We shall take the Book struct as an example:

```go
type Book struct {
    ID     int     `json:"id"`
    Title  string  `json:"title"`
    Author string  `json:"author"`
    Price  float64 `json:"price"`
}
```

In the above, struct tags (like json:"id") indicate how the corresponding struct field should be encoded/decoded to/from JSON.

Encoding Go Data
To convert a Go value to JSON, you can use the json.Marshal function.

```go
book := Book{ID: 1, Title: "Go Basics", Author: "John Doe", Price: 10.99}
jsonData, err := json.Marshal(book)
if err != nil {
    log.Fatalf("Error encoding data: %v", err)
}
fmt.Println(string(jsonData))
```

The result will be a JSON string representing the book's data.

Decoding JSON
Decoding is just as straightforward. Suppose you received a JSON string and wanted to parse it

into a Go struct.

```go
jsonString := `{"id":1,"title":"Go Basics","author":"John Doe","price":10.99}`
var book Book
err := json.Unmarshal([]byte(jsonString), &book)
if err != nil {
    log.Fatalf("Error decoding JSON: %v", err)
}
fmt.Printf("Book Title: %s\n", book.Title)
```

JSON's flexibility allows for nested objects and arrays, letting you represent complex hierarchical data structures. If your Go application involves more intricate data, corresponding nested structs or appropriate data structures (like slices for JSON arrays) will come into play.

Program Data Fetching

Fetching data pertains to retrieving specific pieces of information from a data source, such as a database, and serving it to the user. In modern web applications, the process often involves using RESTful APIs. When we learn data fetching in the context of Go and our bookstore app, we're looking at how to set up an endpoint in the app that will communicate with the database, retrieve the required book data, and then send this data to the user in a specific format, usually JSON.

Setting up Endpoint

Go's net/http package, as learned in previous chapters, makes it straightforward to create HTTP servers and handle requests. To set up an endpoint that fetches book data, we first define a route that maps to a specific function, which will contain our logic to retrieve the data.

```go
http.HandleFunc("/books", getBooks)
http.ListenAndServe(":8080", nil)
```

In the above, we've created a route /books that will trigger the getBooks function when accessed.

Interacting with Database

To fetch data from a database, you would typically use a database driver specific to your database system. For this example, let us assume you're using a SQL database with the database/sql package in Go.

Before fetching, establish a connection:

```go
import (
    _ "github.com/go-sql-driver/mysql"
)

db, err := sql.Open("mysql", "user:password@/dbname")
if err != nil {
    log.Fatal(err)
}
defer db.Close()
```

Now, within the getBooks function, you can query the database:

```go
func getBooks(w http.ResponseWriter, r *http.Request) {
    rows, err := db.Query("SELECT id, title, author, price FROM books")
    if err != nil {
        http.Error(w, err.Error(), http.StatusInternalServerError)
        return
    }
    defer rows.Close()

    var books []Book
    for rows.Next() {
        var b Book
        if err := rows.Scan(&b.ID, &b.Title, &b.Author, &b.Price); err != nil {
            http.Error(w, err.Error(), http.StatusInternalServerError)
            return
        }
        books = append(books, b)
    }

    jsonData, err := json.Marshal(books)
    if err != nil {
        http.Error(w, err.Error(), http.StatusInternalServerError)
        return
```

```
    }

    w.Header().Set("Content-Type", "application/json")
    w.Write(jsonData)
}
```

In the above, the function first queries the database to retrieve all books. It then scans each row of the result into a Book struct and appends it to a slice. Finally, it marshals the slice into a JSON string and writes it to the HTTP response.

While the code above provides a simple example, it's crucial to consider best practices for production-ready applications. This includes using prepared statements for security, managing and reusing database connections efficiently, and handling potential database errors gracefully. Given Go's concurrency capabilities, think about how to utilize goroutines and channels when making multiple simultaneous data fetches, especially if you need to aggregate data from various sources or tables.

Goroutines and Channels for Data Fetching

Why Concurrency in Data Fetching?

Data retrieval often forms the backbone of web applications, particularly those that rely on real-time updates and need to handle substantial traffic. In traditional, synchronous systems, requests for data might be processed one after another. This sequential processing can lead to inefficiencies, especially when some data fetches are time-consuming. Instead of waiting for one operation to complete before starting the next, Go's concurrency model, using goroutines and channels, allows multiple operations to be initiated almost simultaneously, optimizing response times and enhancing user experience.

Also, goroutine is a concurrent function execution that runs independently of other functions and can be thought of as a mini-thread of execution. To spawn a goroutine, simply use the go keyword before a function call:

```
go fetchData("https://api.example.com/data1")
```

However, merely starting goroutines isn't enough. To effectively retrieve data from these concurrent processes, we need a means of communication. Channels provide a way for goroutines to communicate and synchronize. Think of a channel as a pipe where goroutines can send or receive values. Channels ensure safe communication between goroutines and are used to send data from one goroutine to the main program or to other goroutines.

To create a channel:

```
ch := make(chan DataType)
```

Where DataType is the type of data the channel will transmit.

Sample Program: Concurrent Data Fetching

Imagine you need to fetch data from multiple APIs concurrently. Without concurrency, you would send a request to the first API, wait for the data, then send a request to the second, and so on. With goroutines and channels, you can send out multiple requests almost simultaneously and wait for all of them to complete.

Given below is a simplified program:

```go
func fetchData(url string, ch chan<- string) {
    // ... (data fetching logic using net/http or another package)
    ch <- data // Sending fetched data to the channel
}

func main() {
    urls := []string{"https://api1.example.com", "https://api2.example.com"}
    ch := make(chan string, len(urls))

    for _, url := range urls {
        go fetchData(url, ch)
    }

    for range urls {
        data := <-ch
        fmt.Println(data)
    }
}
```

In the above program, the fetchData function retrieves data and sends it to a channel. The main function then reads from the channel and prints out the fetched data.

The combined power of goroutines and channels makes Go especially adept at tasks that benefit from concurrency, like data fetching offering the following benefits:
- Improved Performance: By initiating multiple fetches concurrently, you can drastically reduce the total time required to retrieve all the data.
- Better Resource Utilization: Instead of being idle while waiting for a fetch to complete, the system can initiate other fetches or handle other tasks.

However, while goroutines are lightweight, spawning thousands of them recklessly can overwhelm your system. Always be aware of how many goroutines your application is creating. Concurrent operations can fail independently of each other. It's crucial to implement robust error handling. One common approach is to use a custom struct that holds both the fetched data and any error that occurred:

```
type Result struct {
    Data string
    Err  error
}

ch := make(chan Result)
```

This approach allows each goroutine to send both its fetched data and any error back to the main routine, where appropriate action can be taken.

Authenticating APIs

Importance of API Security

APIs, particularly those handling sensitive or critical data, stand at the forefront of potential cybersecurity threats. This reality is not lost on web applications like the GitforGits Bookstore, where seemingly benign operations could inadvertently become conduits for data breaches or malicious attacks. The possibility of user data leakage, exploitation by bots, or becoming targets for cyber-attacks looms large in the absence of stringent security protocols. Therefore, implementing robust security measures, particularly in API interactions, is not just an enhancement but a necessity. It's crucial to ensure that the data exchanged via APIs remains secure, confidential, and accessible exclusively to authenticated users or systems.

What is API Authentication?

API authentication serves as the gateway to secure interactions, addressing a fundamental question: "Can the identity of a client trying to access the API be verified and trusted?" This process is the cornerstone of API security, acting as the initial barrier against unauthorized access.

Authentication forms the basis upon which more nuanced security measures, such as authorization, are built. While authentication verifies identity, authorization delineates the scope of actions that an authenticated entity is permitted to perform. Together, they form a layered defense mechanism, safeguarding the application's data and functionalities.

Using API Tokens for Authentication

A prevalent and effective strategy for API authentication is the utilization of tokens. These tokens are essentially encrypted strings, unique to each user session, generated by the server upon a user's successful login. This token becomes the user's identifier for subsequent API requests, embedding a layer of security into each transaction. Each token is cryptographically signed, ensuring its integrity and preventing tampering.

When a user initiates a request, the accompanying token undergoes validation, verifying the user's authenticity and granting them the corresponding access. This method is not only secure but also efficient, as it eliminates the need for repeated verifications of the user's credentials. Moreover, token-based authentication aligns seamlessly with stateless protocols, a characteristic intrinsic to modern web applications, thereby enhancing scalability and performance.

Generating and Validating Tokens

A straightforward way to generate tokens in Go is by using JWT (JSON Web Tokens). The github.com/dgrijalva/jwt-go package can assist in creating and verifying JWTs.

Generating a Token

Upon user login or signup, generate a JWT that embeds the user's details, then return this token.

```
import (
        "github.com/dgrijalva/jwt-go"
)

func GenerateToken(userID string) (string, error) {
    token := jwt.NewWithClaims(jwt.SigningMethodHS256, jwt.MapClaims{
       "userID": userID,
    })

    return token.SignedString([]byte("your_secret_key"))
}
```

The token can be decoded to extract the user's details, and its signature ensures it hasn't been tampered with.

Validating Token
For each API request, check the provided token.

```go
func ValidateToken(encodedToken string) (string, error) {
    token, err := jwt.Parse(encodedToken, func(token *jwt.Token) (interface{}, error) {
        return []byte("your_secret_key"), nil
    })

    if claims, ok := token.Claims.(jwt.MapClaims); ok && token.Valid {
        userID := claims["userID"].(string)
        return userID, nil
    }

    return "", err
}
```

Middleware for Authentication
Middleware is a concept where before reaching the actual API handler, the request goes through a series of "middlewares". An authentication middleware can validate tokens for every incoming API request.

```go
func AuthenticationMiddleware(next http.HandlerFunc) http.HandlerFunc {
    return func(w http.ResponseWriter, r *http.Request) {
        token := r.Header.Get("Authorization")
        _, err := ValidateToken(token)
        if err != nil {
            http.Error(w, "Invalid token", http.StatusUnauthorized)
            return
        }
        next(w, r)
    }
}
```

Implementing Middleware
Add the middleware to the routes that need protection.

http.HandleFunc("/protectedEndpoint", AuthenticationMiddleware(HandleProtectedEndpoint))

Using tokens is secure, but there are associated risks. If a token is leaked, it can be misused. It's essential to:
- Use HTTPS: Ensure the API operates over HTTPS. This makes it harder for attackers to intercept tokens.
- Token Expiry: Tokens should have a limited lifespan.
- Handle Breaches: Implement mechanisms to invalidate tokens if you suspect a breach.

Sometimes, it's not about recreating the wheel. Services like Auth0 or Okta provide robust authentication solutions that can be easily integrated into Go applications. They handle user registration, login, and token generation.

Integrate External APIs
Modern web applications often require functionalities that can be better served by specialized external services. Rather than reinventing the wheel, leveraging third-party APIs or services can provide efficient, scalable, and updated solutions. Imagine the need for payment processing, book reviews, or even integrating with a service that provides book summaries or author interviews. External APIs play a pivotal role in enhancing the app's functionalities and improving the user experience.

Choose and Communicate Third-Party API
When considering an external service, it's essential to evaluate its reliability, cost, scalability, and compatibility with your application's needs. Documentation quality, community support, and the provider's reputation are also critical. For our Bookstore app, if we were looking for book reviews, we might consider APIs like Goodreads or a book metadata API like Open Library.

Go's standard library provides robust tools to communicate with external APIs. The net/http package, which we've explored earlier, can be used to send requests and handle responses from these APIs. For example, to fetch book reviews from an external service, we'd use:

resp, err := http.Get("https://bookreviewsapi.com/book/{bookID}")

Sample Program: Integration of Payment Gateway

Let us consider Stripe, a popular choice as a payment gateway for our bookstore application::

```go
import (
    "github.com/stripe/stripe-go"
    "github.com/stripe/stripe-go/charge"
)

stripe.Key = "YOUR_SECRET_KEY"

ch, err := charge.New(&stripe.ChargeParams{
    Amount:   stripe.Int64(2000),
    Currency: stripe.String(string(stripe.CurrencyUSD)),
    Source:   &stripe.SourceParams{Token: stripe.String("TOKEN_FROM_CHECKOUT")},
})
```

This code initializes a charge of $20. Handling tokens, customer management, and other features would require more detailed integration.

Suppose there's a third-party service providing book summaries. You could fetch a book's summary like:

```go
func GetBookSummary(bookID string) (string, error) {
    url := fmt.Sprintf("https://booksummaryapi.com/summary/%s", bookID)
    resp, err := http.Get(url)
    if err != nil {
        return "", err
    }
    defer resp.Body.Close()
    body, _ := ioutil.ReadAll(resp.Body)
    return string(body), nil
}
```

Many external services impose limits on how often you can call them to prevent abuse. These can be rate limits (number of calls per time period) or quotas (total number of calls allowed). Using Go's time.Ticker or a library like golang.org/x/time/rate can help in managing these limits effectively.

Summary

This chapter focused on the interdependence of web applications' frontend and backend, emphasizing the critical importance of effective communication between the two. We investigated external services and the significant impact that third-party APIs can have on enhancing an application's capabilities. These APIs provide specialized services without requiring the development of new fundamental systems. In the case of our Bookstore app, this entailed investigating options such as incorporating Goodreads book reviews, Open Library book metadata, and even payment processing systems such as Stripe.

We thoroughly investigated the net/http package of the Go programming language, which is a powerful tool for communicating with external APIs. The development of endpoints to retrieve book details, the seamless integration of a payment gateway, and the retrieval of book summaries from external sources were all part of the practical aspect. The importance of rate limits and quotas was a critical lesson learned. In order to maintain a smooth operation, it is critical to effectively manage the limitations of external services using tools such as Go's time.Ticker or the golang.org/x/time/rate library. Our main topic of learning was ensuring the security of API interactions. We stressed the importance of not hardcoding API keys and instead relying on environment variables for added security.

Finally, the chapter stressed the importance of monitoring third-party API interactions. Consistent logging, especially of errors and unexpected responses, provides developers with useful information for troubleshooting and improving performance. Third-party services are mutable, which includes potential changes to their API structures, pricing, or services. Periodic assessments ensure that the integrated services are up to date and consistently meet the app's specifications.

Chapter 9: Testing and Debugging

Testing and Debugging Overview

Web applications are the cornerstones of businesses, educational platforms, and entertainment outlets and thereby its ubiquity demand is that they must perform flawlessly, offering a seamless user experience. But how can developers ensure that their application stands robust in the face of evolving user demands, changing infrastructures, and unforeseen challenges? The answer lies in rigorous testing and adept debugging.

Testing is not just a phase in the software development lifecycle; it's an ongoing commitment to quality assurance. It's the safety net that catches lapses in code quality, logic flaws, or design oversights. Without testing, deploying a web application is like navigating treacherous waters without a compass. You're likely to encounter setbacks, often at the most inopportune times. Automated tests, such as unit tests, integration tests, and end-to-end tests, are the checkpoints that validate code health and application functionality at various granularities. For instance, unit tests ascertain the correctness of individual units or functions. Simultaneously, integration tests ensure that distinct software modules operate harmoniously when integrated.

If testing is the proactive guardian of application quality, debugging is the reactive counterpart. It's the meticulous art of identifying and rectifying issues within the codebase. While tests give a macro-level view of where problems might lie, debugging dives deep, scouring code lines, logging statements, and system interactions to pinpoint the exact origin of an issue. Tools like Go's built-in debugger or more advanced solutions like Delve provide developers with insights into variable states, control flow, and even memory allocation.

Beyond functional correctness, web applications must provide an optimal user experience. Here, performance testing steps into the limelight. Response times, load handling capacities, and system resilience under stress are metrics that can make or break an application's reputation. By emulating user traffic, performance tests provide insights into bottlenecks, resource leakages, or inefficient algorithms.

In sum, testing and debugging aren't mere chores in the development process. They're the pillars that uphold application integrity, assuring stakeholders and users that the application they interact with is reliable, robust, and resilient.

Go Testing Package
Fundamentals
The built-in testing package within Go holds a special place, functioning as the cornerstone of Go's testing ecosystem. Designed to support automated testing of Go packages, it provides a minimalistic yet powerful interface, making it easy for developers to craft unit tests, benchmarks, and examples.

The testing package revolves around the T and B types, representing test and benchmark cases, respectively. To define a test function, one must create a function with a signature of (t *testing.T), and the framework will execute these test functions in parallel, allowing for concurrent testing.

A basic test can be as straightforward as:

```
func TestSum(t *testing.T) {
    result := sum(2, 3)
    if result != 5 {
        t.Errorf("Expected 5 but got %d", result)
    }
}
```

In the above program, we're testing a hypothetical sum function, ensuring it correctly adds two numbers. The Errorf method logs an error, similar to Printf, indicating a test failure.

Powerful Assertions and Flow Control

Go's standard testing package, while proficient, does not inherently include an assertion library. Assertions are vital in testing as they validate whether a particular condition in the code holds true, and if not, they provide meaningful error messages. Recognizing this need, the Go ecosystem offers a plethora of third-party libraries that enrich the testing experience. Libraries like Testify or GoConvey are popular choices, offering a more expressive syntax for writing tests and a range of assertion functions that make tests more readable and maintainable.

For instance, consider a scenario in the GitforGits Bookstore where you need to test an API endpoint for fetching book details. Using an assertion library like Testify, you could write a test like:

```
func TestFetchBookDetails(t *testing.T) {
    book, err := FetchBookDetails("123456789")
    assert.Nil(t, err)
    assert.Equal(t, "Go Programming", book.Title)
}
```

In this snippet, assert.Nil checks if err is nil, ensuring no error occurred during the fetch operation, and assert.Equal verifies that the fetched book's title is as expected.

Despite the allure of third-party libraries, Go's built-in testing controls are powerful in their own right. The Errorf, Fatalf, and Skipf methods provide essential controls over the flow of test execution. Errorf logs an error but allows the test to continue, which is useful for reporting non-critical issues that do not warrant stopping the test. For instance, if a part of the response is incorrect, but you wish to continue to check other parts:

```
t.Errorf("Expected book title %s, got %s", expectedTitle, book.Title)
```

Conversely, Fatalf is used when an error is critical enough that the test should not proceed further. This might be used in situations where the failure to meet a condition renders the subsequent test steps invalid or irrelevant.

```
if err != nil {
    t.Fatalf("Failed to fetch book details: %v", err)
}
```

Lastly, Skipf allows you to skip certain tests, perhaps when running in specific environments or under certain conditions. It ensures that tests are only run when relevant, saving time and resources.

Performance Benchmarks

Performance is paramount in web applications, and here too, Go's testing package doesn't disappoint. Using the B type, developers can assess the performance of their code:

```
func BenchmarkSum(b *testing.B) {
    for i := 0; i < b.N; i++ {
        sum(2, 3)
    }
}
```

When you run this benchmark, Go will execute the sum function multiple times, determining an average execution time, which aids in detecting potential performance bottlenecks.

Testing Web Applications

While the testing package facilitates testing Go code in general, when applied to web applications, it becomes indispensable. For instance, using the net/http/httptest package alongside testing, developers can craft mock HTTP requests and responses, simulating real-world interactions with their web applications. This synergy ensures that routes, handlers, and middleware in a web application, like our "GitforGits Bookstore," undergo rigorous validation before deployment.

A common pattern in Go testing is the use of table-driven tests. This approach allows developers to define multiple test cases in a structured manner, enhancing test coverage without redundant code:

```go
func TestSum(t *testing.T) {
    tests := []struct {
        a, b, expected int
    }{
        {2, 3, 5},
        {-2, 3, 1},
        {0, 0, 0},
    }

    for _, tt := range tests {
        result := sum(tt.a, tt.b)
        if result != tt.expected {
            t.Errorf("For (%d, %d), expected %d, but got %d", tt.a, tt.b, tt.expected, result)
        }
    }
}
```

This structure is especially useful for web applications where various input scenarios must be tested to ensure reliability.

Initiating Testing
Setting up Environment
It's pivotal to ensure your environment is well-configured. Fortunately, Go's innate support for testing implies that no extra installation is required. All you need is the standard Go toolchain. Ensure you have it installed by running:

```
go version
```

If you see the Go version displayed, you're set. If not, refer to chapter 1 to install the Go toolkit.

Test File Structure

In Go, tests live alongside the code they test. For instance, if you have a Go file named book.go containing functionalities related to books, the corresponding test file would be named book_test.go. This co-location promotes better code organization and makes it easier to find related tests.

Fetching a Book

Imagine we have a function in book.go that fetches a book based on its ISBN:

```go
func FetchBookByISBN(isbn string) (*Book, error) {
    // ... implementation here ...
}
```

We'll now write a test for this function in book_test.go.

```go
package main

import (
    "testing"
)

func TestFetchBookByISBN(t *testing.T) {
    book, err := FetchBookByISBN("1234567890")
    if err != nil {
        t.Fatalf("Expected no error, but got: %v", err)
    }

    if book == nil {
        t.Fatal("Expected a book, but got nil")
    }

    if book.ISBN != "1234567890" {
        t.Errorf("Expected ISBN to be '1234567890', but got '%s'", book.ISBN)
    }
}
```

In the above, we are invoking our function and checking a few conditions: no error should be returned, a book should be retrieved, and the book's ISBN should match the one we requested.

Executing Test

To run your tests, navigate to the directory containing your test file and execute:

go test

This command compiles and runs the tests in the current package. If all tests pass, you will see a message indicating success. If any test fails, details about the failure will be displayed.

Refining Test with Mock Data

To make tests predictable and avoid potential flakiness, it's advisable to use mock data. For our test, instead of fetching a book from a real database, we'd fetch it from a mock datastore.

We shall assume we have a mock function:

```go
func MockFetchBookByISBN(isbn string) (*Book, error) {
    return &Book{ISBN: "1234567890", Title: "Go in Action"}, nil
}
```

To use this mock function in tests, adjust the test function:

```go
func TestFetchBookByISBN(t *testing.T) {
    book, err := MockFetchBookByISBN("1234567890")
    // rest of the test remains unchanged ...
}
```

Now, our test is independent of external data sources, making it more robust.

Enhancing Test

We previously touched on table-driven tests, and they shine in situations like this. You can test multiple ISBNs, expecting different results, without writing separate test functions for each case. Instead, define a table of test cases and iterate over them.

```go
func TestFetchBookByISBN(t *testing.T) {
```

```go
    tests := []struct {
        isbn         string
        expectedISBN string
    }{
        {"1234567890", "1234567890"},
        {"0987654321", "0987654321"},
        // ... add more test cases as needed ...
    }

    for _, tt := range tests {
        book, err := MockFetchBookByISBN(tt.isbn)
        if err != nil {
            t.Fatalf("Expected no error for ISBN '%s', but got: %v", tt.isbn, err)
        }

        if book.ISBN != tt.expectedISBN {
            t.Errorf("For ISBN '%s', expected '%s', but got '%s'", tt.isbn, tt.expectedISBN, book.ISBN)
        }
    }
}
```

Testing is an integral part of Go development, fostering confidence in code quality. Go's built-in testing tools, combined with best practices like using mock data and table-driven tests, allow for comprehensive testing of web applications.

Handling Multiple Test Cases
Table-Driven Testing
Table-driven testing is a pattern in Go that efficiently lets you run multiple scenarios for a given function or method without writing a new test function for each scenario. This method is not only cleaner but also reduces redundant code, making tests easier to read, write, and maintain.

Imagine you're writing tests for a function that adds two numbers. Instead of creating separate test functions for positive numbers, negative numbers, and zeros, you can use table-driven testing.

```go
func TestAdd(t *testing.T) {
    tests := []struct {
        name string
        a, b int
        want int
    }{
        {"add positives", 3, 4, 7},
        {"add negatives", -3, -4, -7},
        {"add mixed", -3, 4, 1},
        {"add zero", 0, 4, 4},
    }

    for _, tt := range tests {
        t.Run(tt.name, func(t *testing.T) {
            got := Add(tt.a, tt.b)
            if got != tt.want {
                t.Errorf("Add(%d, %d) = %d; want %d", tt.a, tt.b, got, tt.want)
            }
        })
    }
}
```

In the above, you define a slice of anonymous structs, each representing a test case. You then range over this slice, running each test. Using t.Run allows for each test case to run independently and provides a clearer output of which test cases pass or fail.

Utilizing Helper Functions

Helper functions can be instrumental in reducing code redundancy, especially when setting up the context for tests or cleaning up after them. For instance, if testing various functionalities of the bookstore app requires initializing a mock database, you could use a helper function to handle that.

```go
func setupMockDatabase() *MockDB {
    db := &MockDB{}
    // ... some setup code ...
```

```
    return db
}

func tearDownMockDatabase(db *MockDB) {
    // ... cleanup code ...
}
```

In your tests, you can call these functions before and after running test cases, ensuring each test has the necessary context and cleanup.

Parallel Testing

Go has in-built support for parallel testing. When tests don't have dependencies and can run simultaneously, marking them as parallel can speed up the total test execution time.

To run tests in parallel, just call t.Parallel() at the beginning of the test.

```
func TestSomeFeature(t *testing.T) {
    t.Parallel()
    // ... rest of the test ...
}
```

Be cautious when using this. Tests that share state or resources can fail unpredictably when run in parallel. Always ensure your tests are isolated from one another.

Subtests

For structuring your tests and sharing setup/teardown code, Go's testing package provides subtests. This feature is especially useful when multiple tests need to share setup and teardown but represent different scenarios or test cases.

```
func TestBookFeatures(t *testing.T) {
    db := setupMockDatabase()
    defer tearDownMockDatabase(db)

    t.Run("test fetch", func(t *testing.T) {
        // Test fetching a book
    })
```

```
        t.Run("test update", func(t *testing.T) {
            // Test updating a book
        })
    }
```

With subtests, you can group related tests under a parent test, ensuring shared setup and teardown run appropriately.

Adopting patterns like table-driven tests and utilizing features like helper functions, parallel testing, and subtests make the testing process, both rigorous and streamlined. As a result, when scaling or modifying the "GitforGits Bookstore" app, these practices offer confidence that the app not only functions as expected but also maintains performance standards.

Mock Dependencies

Introduction to Mocking

when it comes to unit testing, the concept of mocking is a game-changer. It involves simulating the behavior of real-world objects or systems, such as databases, external APIs, or third-party services, which might be impractical or cumbersome to incorporate directly into unit tests. The essence of mocking lies in its ability to create a controlled environment for tests, isolating the unit of work from external dependencies and interactions. This isolation is crucial as it ensures that tests focus solely on the functionality they are meant to evaluate, without being affected by the behavior or state of external systems.

Why Mock Dependencies?

Suppose you're crafting tests for a function that fetches book details from a database. Integrating a real database into these tests would not only complicate the testing process but also transform it into more of an integration test rather than a unit test. This is because the outcome of the tests would then depend on the database's state and behavior. Mocking steps in as a powerful tool in such situations. By simulating the database, you can focus on testing the function's logic independently, ensuring that the tests are reliable, faster, and more focused.

Creating Mock Database

A practical approach to mocking in Go involves the use of interfaces. For example, if your GitforGits application interacts with a database, you would typically define a Database interface that outlines the operations like fetching a book by its ID. In a testing scenario, instead of using a real database, you can implement a MockDatabase that adheres to this Database interface. However, unlike the real database, the MockDatabase doesn't perform actual database operations.

Instead, it uses internally stored data to simulate these operations.

```go
type Database interface {
    FetchBookByID(id int) (Book, error)
}


type MockDatabase struct {
    books []Book
}


func (m *MockDatabase) FetchBookByID(id int) (Book, error) {
    for _, book := range m.books {
        if book.ID == id {
            return book, nil
        }
    }
    return Book{}, fmt.Errorf("Book not found")
}
```

In this setup, the MockDatabase operates on an internal slice of books, mimicking a real database's behavior. This method allows developers to test the functionality of the FetchBookByID function independently of a live database environment. By returning predefined data, the mock ensures that the test's behavior is predictable and consistent, which is crucial for accurate testing outcomes.

Using Mock in Tests

When writing tests, instead of creating an instance of the real database, you'd instantiate the MockDatabase, preload it with data, and pass it to the functions or methods you're testing.

```go
func TestFetchBookDetails(t *testing.T) {
    mockDB := &MockDatabase{
        books: []Book{
            {ID: 1, Name: "Go Basics", Author: "A. Developer"},
        },
    }
}
```

```go
    book, err := FetchBookDetails(mockDB, 1)
    if err != nil || book.Name != "Go Basics" {
        t.Fail()
    }
}
```

Similarly, for mocking external services or APIs, you can create interfaces that represent the operations you perform on those services. Then, for tests, create mock implementations that return predefined data.

Let us say you have a function that fetches book reviews from an external API:

```go
type ReviewAPI interface {
    FetchReviewsForBook(bookID int) ([]Review, error)
}
```

A mock might look like:

```go
type MockReviewAPI struct {
    reviews map[int][]Review
}

func (m *MockReviewAPI) FetchReviewsForBook(bookID int) ([]Review, error) {
    return m.reviews[bookID], nil
}
```

Mocking provides a controlled environment for your tests. You don't have to worry about external services being down or the internet being slow. Every test run is consistent, making failures easier to diagnose. However, it's crucial to remember that while mocks simulate external behaviors, they might not capture every nuance of the real thing. It's still essential to have integration tests, in addition to unit tests, to ensure all parts of your system work together correctly.

Tracing and Logging

Every application, no matter how well coded, can run into unexpected scenarios or erroneous states. For a complex web app like the GitforGits Bookstore, having visibility into application behavior is essential. This is where tracing and logging come into play. While errors give immediate feedback about a problem, logs provide a narrative of the application's operation, helping developers understand events leading up to an issue.

Performing Logging with Go's log

Go's standard library offers a simple logging package, log. This package provides basic logging functionalities that can be easily incorporated into any Go application.

```
import "log"

func fetchBookDetails(bookID int) (Book, error) {
    // ... fetch operation ...
    if err != nil {
        log.Printf("Error fetching book with ID %d: %v", bookID, err)
        return Book{}, err
    }
    return book, nil
}
```

In the above, if the fetch operation encounters an error, a log entry is created detailing the book ID and the error message.

For a web application, it's beneficial to include request-specific details in logs, such as request ID, user ID, or IP address. This contextual information aids in narrowing down issues and understanding user-specific anomalies.

You can use context values to pass this data. For instance, middleware can be used to attach a unique request ID to every incoming request. This ID can then be used in subsequent logging throughout the request's lifecycle.

Integrating Advanced Logging Libraries

While Go's native log package is sufficient for basic logging, the ecosystem offers advanced logging libraries like logrus and zap. These libraries offer structured logging, where logs are created as structured data (like JSON), making them easily parseable and more informative.

For instance, with logrus:

```
import log "github.com/sirupsen/logrus"
```

```go
func init() {
    log.SetFormatter(&log.JSONFormatter{})
    log.SetLevel(log.InfoLevel)
}

func fetchBookDetails(bookID int) (Book, error) {
    // ... fetch operation ...
    if err != nil {
        log.WithFields(log.Fields{
            "bookID": bookID,
            "error":  err,
        }).Error("Failed to fetch book details")
        return Book{}, err
    }
    return book, nil
}
```

This approach yields logs in JSON format, which can be ingested by modern log aggregation tools or platforms like ELK stack or Splunk.

Error Tracing

Beyond logging, tracing allows you to follow a request's path through various microservices or internal functions. Tracing libraries like OpenTracing can be used in Go to establish spans, which represent units of work.

When an error occurs, not only can you log the error, but you can also capture a trace of all operations leading up to the error. This holistic view enables developers to pinpoint bottlenecks, latency issues, or failures in the system.

As the Bookstore app grows, logs can become voluminous. Centralized log management solutions, such as Logstash or Fluentd, help aggregate, filter, and analyze logs. They offer dashboards, alerts, and insights into application behavior.

When integrating such solutions, ensure that the log format (e.g., JSON) from your application matches what these tools expect. Middleware can be utilized to forward logs from the app to these management solutions.

Application Performance Profiling

Profiling is an essential aspect of understanding application performance. By analyzing how a program utilizes resources like CPU and memory, developers can pinpoint performance bottlenecks and optimize accordingly. Go, with its rich toolset, provides native support for various types of profiling, including CPU, memory, and block (synchronization) profiling. For the GitforGits Bookstore application, leveraging these tools can ensure it runs efficiently, offering users a smooth and responsive experience.

CPU Profiling

CPU profiling helps identify functions consuming a significant portion of CPU time. This can spotlight compute-intensive portions of code that might benefit from optimization.

To begin, you'll want to import the necessary package:

```go
import _ "net/http/pprof"
```

Initiate CPU profiling in your main function or just before the section you wish to profile:

```go
f, _ := os.Create("cpu.pprof")
defer f.Close()
pprof.StartCPUProfile(f)
defer pprof.StopCPUProfile()
```

After running your application, you'll get a cpu.pprof file, which can be analyzed using the go tool pprof command. This offers a variety of commands, such as top to view the top functions by CPU usage.

Block Profiling

Block profiling aids in understanding how goroutines synchronize and how they're blocked waiting on channel operations, network IO, or accessing shared memory.
Start block profiling with:

```go
runtime.SetBlockProfileRate(1)
```

And at the point where you wish to save the profile:

```go
f, _ := os.Create("block.pprof")
```

pprof.Lookup("block").WriteTo(f, 0)

The block.pprof file can be examined using go tool pprof to detect potential synchronization bottlenecks in the Bookstore application.

Memory Profiling

Memory profiling can identify places where the application might be using more memory than expected, leading to increased garbage collection or potential memory leaks.

To profile memory usage:

```
f, _ := os.Create("memory.pprof")
pprof.WriteHeapProfile(f)
f.Close()
```

The resulting memory.pprof can be analyzed using go tool pprof. The top command in the pprof tool can help identify functions responsible for the most memory allocations.

Errors and Troubleshooting

Web applications, given their vast and interconnected nature, are prone to various kinds of bugs. These bugs might arise from simple syntax errors, incorrect data handling, inefficient database queries, or even concurrency issues. For developers, understanding these common issues and having a strategy for addressing them is pivotal to the maintenance and optimization of their web application, especially for the GitforGits Bookstore.

N+1 Query Problem

A widespread performance bug in web applications interfacing with databases is the N+1 query problem. For example, when fetching a list of books and their respective authors from a database, an inefficient implementation might query the database once to retrieve the list of books and then once for each book to get its author.

Solution

Instead of multiple queries, an efficient approach is to use a JOIN operation or batch fetching to retrieve all necessary data in fewer queries.

```
// Inefficient way
for _, book := range books {
    author := db.GetAuthorByID(book.AuthorID)
```

```
    book.Author = author
}
```

```
// Efficient way
booksWithAuthors := db.GetBooksWithAuthors()
```

Data Race Conditions

In web applications, especially those leveraging concurrency, data race conditions can arise when multiple operations try to read and modify shared data simultaneously.

Solution

One can use synchronization primitives like mutexes or channels in Go to ensure that shared data is accessed in a thread-safe manner.

```
var mu sync.Mutex

func UpdateBook(book Book) {
    mu.Lock()
    defer mu.Unlock()
    // update book operation
}
```

Memory Leaks

Memory leaks occur when the application allocates memory but fails to release it. Over time, these leaks can accumulate, leading to reduced performance and potential application crashes.

Solution

Go's garbage collector usually handles memory management. Still, developers should be cautious with global variables, un-closed channels, or lingering goroutines. Tools like pprof can help identify memory leaks.

```
// Ensure channels are closed after use
ch := make(chan int)
close(ch)
```

Broken Authentication Flows

Issues in authentication flows, like not properly validating user inputs or failing to handle tokens securely, can lead to security vulnerabilities.

Solution

Always use established libraries for authentication, validate user inputs rigorously, and store sensitive tokens securely.

```
// Validate user input
if username == "" || password == "" {
    return errors.New("username or password cannot be empty")
}
```

Inefficient Data Handling

Processing large amounts of data without pagination or filtering can degrade application performance.

Solution

Implement pagination for large datasets and ensure data filtering occurs at the database level rather than in the application.

```
// Fetching only 10 books at a time
books := db.GetBooks(limit: 10, offset: 0)
```

Input Validation Failures

A common oversight in web applications is not validating or improperly validating user inputs. This can lead to a range of issues, from unexpected application behavior to severe security vulnerabilities like SQL Injection or Cross-Site Scripting (XSS).

Solution

Always validate user inputs rigorously before processing. Avoid placing raw user input directly into queries or displaying it without sanitization.

```
// Basic input validation
if len(bookTitle) < 3 {
    return errors.New("book title is too short")
```

}

Incorrect Error Handling

Not handling errors correctly can either crash the application or expose sensitive information to the end-users. Sometimes developers might unintentionally expose stack traces, revealing potential application vulnerabilities.

Solution

Always catch and handle errors. Instead of exposing raw error messages, display a generic message to the user and log the detailed error for developer reference.

```
err := db.SaveBook(book)
if err != nil {
    log.Println("Error saving book:", err)
    return errors.New("failed to save the book")
}
```

Dependency Update Failure

Web applications often rely on external libraries or frameworks. Bugs or vulnerabilities in these dependencies can affect the application's security and performance.

Solution

Regularly update the application's dependencies. Use tools that can automatically check for outdated or vulnerable libraries.

```
// Use tools like 'go get -u' to update Go dependencies
```

Hardcoding Configuration

Hardcoding configurations like database credentials, API keys, or other sensitive data directly into the application's code can lead to security risks, especially if the codebase is publicly accessible.

Solution

Use environment variables or configuration files that are not committed to the code repository. Tools like Go's os package can fetch environment variables easily.

```
dbPassword := os.Getenv("DB_PASSWORD")
```

Unsafe Concurrency Handling

Given Go's strong concurrency capabilities with goroutines, it's easy to fall into the trap of unsafe concurrent access to shared resources.

Solution

Always ensure safe concurrent access, either by using channels or synchronization mechanisms like mutexes.

```go
var countMutex sync.Mutex

func IncrementCount() {
  countMutex.Lock()
  defer countMutex.Unlock()
  count++
}
```

A robust testing regimen, combined with an understanding of common pitfalls, can greatly enhance the reliability and security of applications like our GitforGits Bookstore. Being proactive in identifying and fixing these bugs is key to maintaining a high-quality application.

Summary

This chapter thoroughly examined the complex aspects of testing and debugging for web applications, emphasizing their critical role in ensuring software quality and dependability. We began our process by recognizing the critical importance of both testing and debugging. Without these practices, any application is vulnerable to inconsistencies, unexpected behavior, and security flaws. Testing ensures that our code works as intended, whereas debugging aids in detecting and resolving any unexpected issues that may have slipped through our tests.

Understanding the complexities of Go's testing package was critical to our journey. We learned how it creates a stable foundation for creating and executing tests, bolstering our efforts to ensure the Bookstore application's resilience in the face of various scenarios. The practical exercises guided us through the process of writing and running our first tests, emphasizing the importance of testing in ensuring the robustness of our application in the face of potential challenges. Furthermore, we addressed the domain of efficient multiple test cases, ensuring complete coverage of all functions and methods.

Another critical component was the practice of mocking dependencies. Dependencies such as databases or external services are critical in practical scenarios such as the Bookstore. Nonetheless, during the testing phase, we would prefer to replicate these interdependencies rather than use the actual ones. Mocking aided in the achievement of this goal by ensuring that our tests were expedited and protected from outside influences. Furthermore, we thoroughly investigated advanced debugging techniques such as error tracing, logging, and application profiling. To achieve peak performance, it is critical to analyze and comprehend the application's CPU, block, and memory usage patterns.

Finally, in any chapter on debugging, it is critical to learn common bugs that frequently affect web applications. We investigated a wide range of potential issues, including flaws in input validation and error handling, as well as specific challenges associated with concurrency in Go. Understanding and resolving these common issues not only improves the functionality of our Bookstore application, but also provides us with the knowledge to avoid similar challenges in future endeavors. This chapter reinforced the idea that, while coding is a creative endeavor, the ability to thoroughly test and debug code is equally important in web application development.

Thank You

Index

A

API 24, 25, 35, 36, 42, 58, 128, 129, 136, 137, 138, 139, 140, 142, 145, 155, 162
Authentication 12, 113, 119, 137, 138, 139, 161

B

Backend 126, 127
Block profiling 158

C

Cache 107
Concurrency 98, 99, 109, 110, 111, 112, 135, 163
Configuration....................25, 33, 35, 36, 37, 162
CPU profiling 158
CPU, block, and memory 164
CRUD operations 13, 64

D

Debugging 80, 81, 143, 144
Dependency 6, 22, 38, 39, 42
Dynamic 48, 49, 52, 67, 73
Dynamic rendering 67

E

Endpoints...40, 53
External APIs...140

F

Fetching data...133
Forms..75
Frontend 126, 127

G

Gorilla Mux...2, 9, 11
Goroutines 99, 100, 101, 102, 103, 104, 105, 106, 110, 111, 135
Grouping routes 53

H

Handlers...11, 35, 46
HTTP request........4, 10, 11, 16, 32, 44, 46, 64, 130, 146

I

Indexing 91

J

JSON 16, 46, 62, 128, 129, 130, 131, 132, 133, 135, 138, 156, 157

L

Logging 120, 155, 156
Loops..68

M

Memory profiling 159
Mocking...153, 155, 164
Modules 2, 6, 8, 9, 21, 22, 27, 28, 29, 30
MVC..30, 31, 32

N

net/http package 10, 11, 12, 15, 17, 19, 30, 46, 64, 76, 127, 129, 133, 140, 142

O

OAuth 123, 124, 125

P

Profiling..158, 159

R

Rate limiting..59
RESTful 14, 15, 16, 128, 129, 133
Routes.............................33, 34, 35, 48, 49, 53, 55, 64
Routing 11, 43, 44, 45, 48, 49, 50, 55, 56

S

Safe HTML rendering 78
Secure cookie 117
SQL 16, 25, 39, 40, 85, 86, 90, 94, 97, 133, 161
SQL queries 86, 90, 97
sync.Mutex 104, 105, 106, 107, 111, 112, 160, 163
sync.WaitGroup 104, 105, 106
Synchronization 104

T

Template 77, 80

Testing 7, 131, 143, 144, 146, 147, 150, 152, 163

U

URL parameters 51, 52, 53, 64
User Session 114, 120

V

Variables 35, 36, 49, 51, 68

Epilogue

As our time together in "Web Programming with Go" comes to a close, we are nearing the end of an exciting new chapter in the history of webpage development. One that is sleeker, faster, and more resilient, guided by Go. But, like with any epic journey, the finale is only the beginning. The enormous sea of Go's potential awaits you, and with this book's expertise, you'll be able to sail its every wave and current.

The digital fabric of our times is in constant motion, and the hunt for developers to adapt and progress is never-ending. You've selected a formidable ally by including Go in your toolkit. A friend that simplifies where others confuse, scales where others fail, and endures when others fade. Didn't our 'bookstore app' bear witness to this? It reflected the revolutionary force of Go in web development from its humble beginnings to its complicated evolutions.

However, keep in mind that technology is, at its core, a tool. Its actual potential can be realized not only by comprehending its grammar or structure, but also by imagining its prospective applications. "Web Programming with Go" laid the groundwork, but it is on this foundation that you will construct, create, and shape the future. Go is an excellent fit for this because of its simplicity, concurrency architecture, and embracing of current computing principles. But the artistry of what you create is all your own.

Another important realization is that learning is an iterative process. The web development landscape is peppered with constant developments, evolutions, and revolutions. The ecosystem that surrounds Go will flourish as it grows in popularity and application. New libraries will spring up, paradigms will shift, and best practices will emerge. The onus is on us, the Go developer community, to remain lifelong learners, to keep up with these developments, and, most importantly, to contribute to the growing corpus of Go's knowledge.

Furthermore, we must not lose sight of the core of Go, which surpasses its technical prowess. It's a language that arose from a necessity, a gap, or an inefficiency in the current quo. It's an example of necessity-driven invention. Remember to be problem solvers first and coders second as you use the power of Go. Identify gaps, imagine answers, and utilize Go to connect them. Whether it's improving backend processes, integrating complex APIs, or simply developing previously unthinkable user experiences, let Go be your canvas and innovation your brush.

In retrospect, even though we dug deep into Go's libraries, functions, and intricacies, the most powerful takeaway from this book should be an attitude - a mindset of simplicity, efficiency, and invention. A mindset that does not avoid challenges, but instead meets them with the strength of Go. Blending this attitude with your unique insights, ideas, and experiences will be the game changer as you move forward.

Finally, as you finish this book, remember that you've gained more than just an understanding of a programming language. You have a philosophy, a vision, and a capability. The world of online programming is broad and frequently difficult, but with Go as your chosen tool and the information from "Web Programming with Go" as your guide, the horizon has never looked brighter.

The adventure with Go has only just begun. Have fun exploring!

Made in the USA
Monee, IL
03 May 2026